OBJECT LESSONS

A book series about the hidden lives of ordinary things.

Series Editors:

Ian Bogost and Christopher Schaberg

D1745023

In association with

Program *in* Public Scholarship

Washington University in St. Louis

BOOKS IN THE SERIES

Relic

ED SIMON

BLOOMSBURY ACADEMIC
NEW YORK • LONDON • OXFORD • NEW DELHI • SYDNEY

BLOOMSBURY ACADEMIC
Bloomsbury Publishing Inc
1385 Broadway, New York, NY 10018, USA
50 Bedford Square, London, WC1B 3DP, UK
29 Earlsfort Terrace, Dublin 2, Ireland

BLOOMSBURY, BLOOMSBURY ACADEMIC and the Diana logo are trademarks of
Bloomsbury Publishing Plc

First published in the United States of America 2024

Copyright © Ed Simon, 2024

Cover design: Alice Marwick

Bloomsbury Publishing Inc does not have any control over, or responsibility for, any
third-party websites referred to or in this book. All internet addresses given in this
book were correct at the time of going to press. The author and publisher regret
any inconvenience caused if addresses have changed or sites have ceased to exist,
but can accept no responsibility for any such changes.

Whilst every effort has been made to locate copyright holders the publishers would
be grateful to hear from any person(s) not here acknowledged.

A catalog record for this book is available from the Library of Congress

ISBN: PB: 979-8-7651-0228-2
ePDF: 979-8-7651-0230-5
eBook: 979-8-7651-0229-9

Series: Object Lessons

Typeset by Deanta Global Publishing Services, Chennai, India
Printed and bound in Great Britain

To find out more about our authors and books visit www.bloomsbury.com and
sign up for our newsletters.

"There are moments when the body is as numinous / as words, days that are the good flesh continuing."
- Robert Hass, "Meditation at Lagunitas"

CONTENTS

INTRODUCTION— THESES ON THE HOLY FACE

Inhabitants of Manoppello have long maintained that the miraculous image of Christ's battered face kept within the Capuchin friary of Satuario del Volto Santo—rendered in a patina of unknown origin upon preposterously fragile silk woven from the filaments of Mediterranean mollusks—was brought to the mountainous village by a mysterious pilgrim in 1508 who deposited the shroud with a local physician, and then promptly vanished, though cynics may note that the portrait had conveniently gone missing from the Vatican two years before. For five centuries, without the wider world much noticing or caring, the image has been preserved under glass and framed in bronze, and Christ has stared out at the congregation with exhausted russet eyes, his nose bulbous and broken, his brown hair hanging languid and limp, his gaping mouth without the trace of a smile. Despite the hair and beard, the messiah appears completely unlike the shining icon we've been conditioned to see him as—none of the stereotypical and ahistorical Nordic physiognomy, none of the perfected physique. There is a shocking verisimilitude—the savior between his beating and his crucifixion—appearing as if you could smell the salt of blood and sweat sticking to him, a body contorted by torture until the mind becomes synonymous with the soul. More defeated than triumphant. His grotesquerie is beautiful; his ugliness is sacred. Believers in the face maintain that it is Veronica's Veil; that to gaze upon it is to see the actual face of Christ. That it's an ugly face makes it all the truer.

Peter Manseau writes of relics in *Rag and Bone: A Journey Among the World's Holy Dead* that such objects "make explicit what we all know in our bones: that bodies tell stories; that the transformation offered by faith is not just about, as the Gospels put it, the 'word made flesh,' but the flesh made word." Far less celebrated than the similar (though less stunning) shroud six hundred miles to the north in Turin, the Holy Face of Manoppello speaks to the sacredness of physicality, the strange and unlikely experience of what it means to exist— for a time—in a body. When my parents visited Manoppello in 1973, ascending the long, scrubby peak upon which Volto Santo sits, the local priest and several of the villagers gathered to watch their slow climb. After they arrived, the priest asked if they were there to "see the miracle?" They were not—this was the village of my grandfather's birth and where he was reared (like generations of his family) until emigrating as an adolescent in the years before the First World War, and my mother had come to finally see this place. Still, once you've been asked if you want to see a miracle, who among us would be able to say no? My mother knew about the Holy Face of Manoppello, of course. My grandfather Edward, despite being of a largely skeptical and easy-going caste of mind regarding issues of faith (a stereotype about Italian men even a century ago), knew all of the legends regarding the icon—that it had been left by an errant crusader knight travelling through Abruzzi, that it was gifted by an angel. Regardless of the face's provenance, in Manoppello it had been a basic facet of the village experience for centuries. Long before its rediscovery in the past few decades by a whole segment of the Church—the features on EWTN, the account of Pope Benedict XVI praying before it— the veil was simply the miracle a few homes over. My grandfather would have been baptized before the face of Christ, would have taken his first Communion before the face of Christ, would have confessed, been confirmed, and received the Eucharist before the face of Christ. His father would have marked his life before the face of Christ. His grandfather. His great-grandfather. Back to whatever errant crusader knight or angel dropped the Holy Face of Manoppello there in the Capuchin friary of Satuario del Volto Santo.

Because I've long been haunted by the face (albeit a benign possession as far as these things go), I've wanted to make the icon, and relics more generally, a hinge of some sort of narrative, which in my own incomplete and perhaps incompetent way I'm finally attempting now. What haunts me is this sense that to look at the Christ of Manoppello is to be confronted with the beautiful paradox of Catholicism, of Christianity, this myth about man becoming God and then dying as we all do. Generations immemorial in the village conducted their lives in the proverbial presence of the miracle, they raised families and reared animals before it, they grilled arrosticini and porchetta in the same town where Christ's funeral shroud was kept, they built stone walls and drew water from mountain wells before the face of God—all of that says something ineffable about how close the sacred and the profane are. Something ineffable that if it were possible to circumscribe with language would be able to succinctly state my own beliefs, or at least I think it would. Americans, enraptured as they are to that Protestant sentiment which holds membership in a religion as being an ascension to a checklist of postulates tend to see faith as a binary issue of definition—you either are or aren't something, you either believe or you don't. But if anything has motivated my own fascination with religion, and certainly my writing about it, it's been a rejection of that dichotomy. Atheist? Believer? The Question itself is boring.

I'm neither trying to be cagey or cute—I suppose that most of the time I don't believe, but that often I do. When it comes to creeds, my own religion (separate from faith or belief) could be described by the Kingsley Amis quip in *One Fat Englishmen,* that "He was of the faith chiefly in the sense that the church he currently did not attend was Catholic." In my understanding, the *Pater Noster* is more enigma than prayer, the *Ave Maria* poetry as much as supplication. Still, we are what we are. If religion is defined simply as the attempt to uncover whatever it is that gives ultimate meaning, then I confess I want to be as much a pilgrim as the most pious of us, though my path is confusing (most of all to myself). Regardless of whether we believe or not, I've found that those circumstances can change within the period of a few minutes, I've still seen the shadows of faith in everything from the State of the Union address to the Superbowl and I see them more in objects than I do mere ideas. Such an approach of ecumenical promiscuity informs this book, because if there is a central claim, it's that there is a type of *relic logic* which animates our sense of how materiality can mean more than itself, whether in a church or a museum, a monument or a graveyard. Relic logic is perhaps most obvious among the faithful, though certainly many religions or interpretations of religions reject the concrete for the abstract, the physical for the austere, the sensual for the ascetic. Yet my personal understanding of faith has always been estimably fleshy, for I'm not sure if God is in His heaven or not, but I know that we're all here on Earth. I know that we're all equally condemned and blessed to exist within a body, capable of sublime pleasure and hideous suffering, and that all ethics must come from this inviolate truth.

I've long suspected, or maybe imagined, or wished, or pretended, that if I could properly describe the face at Manoppello, that if I was able to theorize myself into some sort of position on what the icon means, that I'd be able to formulate my own *ars theopoetica,* some personal doxology that summarizes all of the inchoate things I've argued about faith. Mostly I feel some proprietary ownership over God's face, far away in a village I've never seen in a country which I've never visited. What attracts me to the bruised, bloated, battered face of Manoppello is a sense of the embodied numinous, the sacredness of physicality. Surveying what I've written, what I've argued about, what I've thought, I seem perennially fixated on what it means to be a person composed of animate matter, the sort of perseveration that shouldn't be unexpected for a recovering alcoholic who watched his father die of bone cancer. Consistently uncomfortable in my own flabby skin, and fully cognoscente of how much of faith is of the body rather than the soul (for at least I know the former exists), I think the face whispers something about suffering and comfort, pain and ecstasy. For as much as Catholicism is configured as otherworldly, all of those mystics and saints, it's very much a faith enmeshed in material reality as well, or maybe the way in which the atoms of heaven and earth can't help but be mingled together. Like many Catholics, I imagine, the reasoning of transubstantiation completely escapes me, but the poetry is unassailable. In part that's because, like those ancestors laboring in the hot Abruzzese sun, hands calloused and cracked sifting through the red soil of the earth, feet aching as they stumble over rocky soil after a long day, I've always been too poor a mystic to dismiss the bodily. So much about God depends on if we're hungry, or anxious, or lonely, or tired. And if we've got to shit, for that matter.

Critic Terry Eagleton, in a reading of the Catholic poet Gerard Manley Hopkins included in *How to Read a Poem,* argues that the priest's verse avoids "two heretical extremes: on the one hand, the radical Protestant view that grace and Nature are absolutely at odds with one another, and on the other hand what is known as the Pelagian heresy, for which grace is natural to us." Strung between Protestant Geneva and pagan Athens, I've eschewed falling into the postlapsarian despair of the former and the lusty pantheism of the latter, acknowledging that ours is a cracked and fallen world, but oh, it still has such beauty in it. That's not dogma, however, it's sentiment. Perhaps having rejected both Geneva and Athens, that's Catholic Pittsburgh for me (more modest than Rome, but just as holy).

By any estimation, I'm a pretty bad Catholic. Yet an unmistakable Catholic sensibility animates my writing, for mine is the piety of the crucifix, but not the cross; belief in Friday but skepticism about Sunday. Catholic is what the Church says I am, and I don't have it in me to argue otherwise. Besides, the evidence is besmeared through my soul like ashes on a forehead. "Grace is not spontaneous," writes Eagleton, "but neither is it arbitrary. It does not already suffuse the world, but it's not alien to it either." Regardless of my ever-variable positions on metaphysics, the substance of that observation seems about right to me. Despite a bit of theological anarchism, and contrary to any sense of personal disinterestedness about the subject, I've always written about faith for one reason—neither for analysis or interpretation, understanding or knowledge—but for *transcendence*. The thing to remember about transcendence, however, is that it may be imparted to the soul, but it's always felt in the body. A theology of materiality strikes me as the only theology of which we can say anything definite.

I affirm that materialism pushed to its logical conclusion arrives back at mysticism; it preserves its idealism in a circumlocutory manner. After all, there is nothing intrinsically less mysterious about an electron than there is about the soul and there is something far more real about flesh and blood than mere spirit, though just as unusual. So familiar are we with the experience of having a body, that its sheer strangeness goes unremarked upon (as is the want of such things). When it comes to the relationship between flesh and spirit, I think of that great libertine saint, that wondrous fallen holy man Oscar Wilde. After his conversion to Catholicism, Wilde was asked by his friend Robert Ross if he actually thought there was legitimacy in the theology of the Church, to which he responded "No, Robbie, it isn't true." The anecdote has always struck me as exceedingly beautiful, the dying aesthete drawing succor from a Church he didn't even believe in. If there is anything that I see in the eyes of the face of Manoppello it's that: an intimation of things beyond that which we can see, hear, touch, smell, taste, yet is somehow still fully enmeshed in the blessed mystery of the physical, just as otherworldly as the spiritual. It's something far beyond prosaic data. Nothing seems inconsistent to me in giving yourself over to a set of beliefs that you feel not to be true, because it seems to me that faith is larger than mere fact. Like Wilde, I may doubt God's existence, but I've never doubted His love.

1 RELIGION

"*I sing the body electric ...*
The man's body is sacred and the woman's body is
sacred,
No matter who it is, it is sacred."
— WALT WHITMAN, *LEAVES OF GRASS* (1855)

A master of chiaroscuro almost the equal of the great Caravaggio, the Spanish baroque painter Francisco de Zurbarán was able to render compositions of stunning intensity—fruit which glows in *Still Life with Lemons, Oranges and a Rose;* four simple receptacles in *Still Life with Pots,* including two white ceramic pitchers, a golden cup on a pewter saucer, and a rough-hewn red clay olive oil pourer; the otherworldly eeriness of a pristine white lamb bound for sacrifice in the unsettling *Agnus Dei.* In keeping with the elan Vitale of chiaroscuro, each of his primary subjects in those paintings appears lit by an otherworldly inner luminescence against the pitch-black background. Visually, such contrast is an expression of the difference and similitude between the sacred and the profane, the intermingling of body and spirit, but as true faith is also always intermingled with doubt, there is an ambiguity in teasing out the borders between these various realms. Baroque artists, inheritors of that Counter-Reformation aesthetic theory which endowed the base materiality of painting and sculpture with a trace of divine immanence, understood that the striking contrasts of light and dark which define chiaroscuro were particularly suitable in the rendering of sacred subjects, and Zurbarán was no exception. The Immaculate Conception, the Annunciation, and the Crucifixion were all depicted by Zurbarán, as were the martyrdoms and passions of saints from Sebastian to Francis. Particularly instructive in Zurbarán's method is his *Apparition of the Child Jesus to Saint Anthony of Padua,* painted between 1627 and 1630, with the original held by the Sao Paulo Museum of Art in Brazil, completed some four centuries after the Portuguese Franciscan died in the Italian countryside from the convulsions of ergotism developed after ingesting bread that had molded with toxic fungus.

As imagined by Zurbarán, Anthony is a lean, almost gaunt figure in his fourth decade of life, supplicating upon his knees in a simple brown cowl, the hood of his robe covering his tonsured pate, with his thin goateed face looking upward in a rapturous intensity, hands held in prayer. Zurbarán's Anthony is handsome, with an expression that could almost be described as equal parts ecstatic and threatening, a tough man who nonetheless kneels open-mouthed in adoration before the mystical vision of the infant Christ floating in the otherwise undifferentiated field of black which constitutes the medium of their setting. *Apparition of the Child Jesus to Saint Anthony of Padua* has as its subject materiality: the relationship of our bodies to the transcendent. The bend of the knee and the clasping of wrists, the strained eye and the grimaced face, all in rapture before the divine, which itself appears in the form of a physical child. Just as Catholicism is defined by the paradox of incarnation, of God becoming a man, so too does art convey something of the strange interdependence of matter and spirit, for Zurbarán's composition which so masterfully presents the viewer with the illusion of being before Anthony is but oil dabbed onto canvas. Confronting Zurbarán's canvas in Sao Paulo, it's apt to consider the critic John Berger's observation in *Ways of Seeing* that the "visual arts have always existed at a certain preserve; originally the preserve was magical or sacred," so that there is a direct connection between aesthetics and the relics, even more so because both were "also physical… The experience of art, which at first was the experience of ritual," based in the materiality of such objects. God may not be approachable, but a relic can be touched, handled, caressed, kissed, fondled.

Incidentally, if you desire to see not just a painting of the saint, but the real thing, Anthony's body survives in pieces, held within the ornate reliquaries designed for the physical remnants of those whose souls didn't require the cleansing fires of purgatory upon death, rather finding themselves directly in heaven through merit of their own goodness and faith. These are First-class relics, that is pieces of the saint's actual body, to be contrasted with Second-class relics which are objects owned by a saint (rosaries, crucifix), and Third-class relics which are merely any prosaic thing which happens to have been in contact with the first two varieties of sacred objects. What's left of the monk—a First-class relic—is largely confined to the magnificent Romanesque Basilica of Saint Anthony of Padua in Veneto, a structure assembled over the centuries out of various styles as surely as its namesake's body was pulled apart.

Celebrated for his rhetorical eloquence and his scholastic brilliance while alive, even by the humble founder of the Franciscan order who tended to be skeptical of such things, the basilica keeps preserved Anthony's trachea, a portion of his chin, and his tongue—all of the instruments of his preaching. Once these organs expressed the living gospel to penitents and the powerful, heretics and the faithful, and, according to one miracle recounted in hagiography, to a school of fish along the Marecchia River. Now those bits of cartilage are dormant, framed in gild and jewels near the altar of the basilica which bears his name. Anthony's skull remains, jawless and charred by entropy, sitting upon a red velvet pillow behind glass alongside an assortment of other bones, a femur here and a bit of spinal cord there, some ribs and an arm. Victim of time and servant of decomposition just like everybody else, the tawny skin which had once covered this skull wasted away, along with all of Anthony's muscles and ligaments. The buccinator, the lateral pterygoid, the masseter, and the media pterygoid all slick with rot, ultimately turned to dust; his eyes (whether brown, or green, or blue) finally disengaged of their vitreous gel, corneas, retinas, and nerves all decayed away, everything gone, vanity of vanities and all the rest.

Staring into the fathomless void of Anthony's eye sockets, the pilgrim isn't just forced to grapple with death, but also the diving mystery of all living faces, the anatomy of his being now erased to leave behind that gleaming skull, an icon of base materiality that when animated by some energy of life was once able to move, and talk, and think. "But man is a Noble Animal," writes the English physician Thomas Browne in his 1658 *Hydriotaphia, or Urn-Burial,* his reflection on the earthly remains of cremated Anglo-Saxons discovered within a series of pots in an English field. Browne writes that humans are "splendid in ashes, and pompous in the grave, solemnizing Nativities and Deaths with equal lustre, nor omitting Ceremonies of Bravery, in the infamy of his nature."

A Protestant of latitudinarian inclinations, Browne was not necessarily a man to conventionally venerate relics himself, but he understood the impulse. He knew that corpses have as much to tell us as the living do, and Anthony is no exception. For example, Anthony was taller than average for the time, around 5'6", perhaps a nutritional benefit of being raised by a father who was a knight in the service of King Alfonso of Portugal. His feet are flattened and hobbled, the result of being a mendicant monk in Morocco and Provence,

Portugal and Spain, Sicily and Assisi. Most notably, his shin bones were permanently indented, a life lived on bended knee. Faith is a matter of the spirit but its effects are rendered on the body. Relics remind us of that. They also remind us of something else Browne wrote—"Life is a pure flame, and we live by an invisible Sun within us."

Saint or not, Anthony's physical fate is the same as all the rest of us fallen creatures in this fallen world—death and decay. Except, matter is never entirely without spirit, because just as the spiritual must always intersect with the material, the corpse of a saint is never just a memento mori focusing our minds towards death, but also a conduit to the sacred calling us towards things beyond this world, a bit of the holy inserted into the profane. "We must not forget that, while the relic might be discovered, transferred, installed, and the annual memory of the saint celebrated in an atmosphere of high ceremony associated with unambiguously good happenings," writes Peter Brown in *The Cult of the Saints: Its Rise and Function in Latin Christianity*, "the relic itself still carries with it the dark shadows of its origin: the invisible person" of the saint. These objects then are marked by the reality that all of us have organs and bones, blood and flesh, but that relics are the organs, bones, blood, and flesh of *saints*. For it was discovered upon exhumation of his remains in 1263, slightly more than three decades after his death, that despite the inevitable decomposition that afflicts most people, and had indeed affected most of Anthony's body, his wet tongue remained incorruptible, as slick and sinewy as when he'd preached the gospel to men and fishes alike. And so, his lower jaw and chin were separated from the rest of his lonely skull along with the tough bit of muscle that had once so eloquently moved in service of the Lord, now placed into an ornate, golden reliquary. His jaw sits behind a bit of curved glass which replaces a face on a golden stand in the shape a pair of shoulders, the head of the figure crowned with a bejeweled halo the color of topaz and rubies. The tongue is displayed in a separate reliquary, appearing as if an untenderized bit of meat scarcely recognizable as having once been human, though at least identifiably flesh. An incorruptible tongue, the faithful believing that its miraculous preservation means that (proverbially) it's still able to speak of the promise of resurrection nearly a millennium later.

Faith isn't the only means of restoring the dead, for attempts were made in the twentieth century to call upon the sophisticated tools of forensic science to ascertain what the saint looked like. The most recent effort, in 2012, was conducted by the Brazilian facial reconstruction expert Cicero Moraes, who used a mold of the saint's skull to try and resurrect at least the appearance of Anthony from the other side of death. Layering onto a plastic skull grey clay etched with lines imitating musculature, Moraes recomposed the saint, reapplying buccinator, lateral pterygoid, masseter, and the media pterygoid, reinserting eyes (though they can't see) and a tongue (though it can't speak). The result is a man bearing little similarity to the smoldering sensuality of Zurbarán's baroque sensibilities, rather a portly and pleasant appearing deacon, a pudgy and smiling olive-complexioned gentleman in his mid-30s with a thin and long nose and kind brown eyes.

"Many times, people look at relics and don't make the connection," Moraes told reporters, "but when there's a face, the person stops to look at the image with more humanity." I don't entirely agree. It's rightly fair to surmise that viewers find something remarkable in the conjuration of Anthony with a 3D scanner and some clay, but despite the oddity and arguably the horror of an object such as a tongue in a gold case, I still very much see the human in the relic. More of the human, in fact, for Moraes's recreation is merely an educated best guess, whereas the blackened stump of a tongue in Padua is the actual flesh that not only preached before Pope Gregory IX (who called Anthony a "jewel case of the Bible") but that also suckled at his mother's breast and that drank from fresh springs, which masticated bread and cheese, and partook in the Eucharist. Within this gilded chamber is the tongue which moved against the palette and the teeth, which pronounced plosives and fricatives, sibilants and rhotics, consonants and vowels, all to preach that "The life of the body is the soul." Relics also demonstrate the inversion of that axiom.

Preaching was Anthony's art, his ability to conjure intricate understandings from the simple combination of air and the movement of the tongue, perhaps the movement of the arm. A living demonstration of how the spiritual can be rendered from the physical. Such learned piety is what led to

Anthony's canonization in 1232, a year after his death, as well as his being declared a Doctor of the Church in the twentieth century, alongside only thirty-six other women and men. "If, then, thou seekest miracles," wrote Julian of Speyer in a 1235 hymn to Anthony entitled *The Raccolta,* "Death, error, all calamities, / the leprosy and demons flee, / The sick, by him made whole, arise."

A particular burden of every saint is that they have multiple responsibilities, so that Anthony's domain includes being a patron of travelers, pregnancy, the harvest, the disabled, the elderly, and the hungry (all estimably material matters), as well as specializing in more niche positions, such as being both the patron saint of mailmen and swineherds. Most famously, St. Anthony is the patron of those who've lost something, his intercession called upon in the recovery of things which can't be found. The origin of this unusual though useful ability—which has long ensured Anthony's popularity— is his recovery of a stolen psalter while he was staying in a monastery, alongside the successful imploration for the thief to repent and join the order. Since his association with lost things, Anthony has been enlisted in the recovery of wedding rings and remote controls, car keys and wallets. The skeptic might mock such minor miracles, though the everyday religion of the everyday person understands that "faith" and "grace" are concepts for preachers and theologians, but that for the rest of us much rests on a wallet and our car keys. With some irony it could be noted that within the jawbone of Anthony there is a single tooth of the saint missing.

Not all saints endure as relics, but every Catholic relic has some connection to a saint, or a member of the Holy Family, or a prophet, or a patriarch. In some ways relics were the original art objects of Western civilization, not in the mundane sense that reliquaries were often beautiful works of craftsmanship (though they often are), but because just like a painting rendered from mere canvas and oil, so too does the bone and flesh of the relic have a value that far exceeds its literal composition. Unlike wheat and millet, which serves a clear instrumental purpose, a relic has value because it's been decided that it has value, not so different from a Van Gogh, or a Picasso, or a Warhol today. And just as a network of tourists make their trips to the Prado, the Uffizi, and the Louvre, so too were Medieval European pilgrimage sites linked together, thousands of travelers make their way through Santiago de Compostello, or Canterbury, or Jerusalem to view a piece of the true cross or a bit of vestment, a finger bone or a vial of uncoagulated blood. Edith L.B. Turner and Victor Turner write, in *Image and Pilgrimage in Christian Culture*, how the circuit of pilgrimage "had an important, but much neglected, impact on future economic and political, as well as religious, developments." Churches and cathedrals, monasteries and abbeys, basilicas and chapels which held relics could "exert a magnetic effect on the whole communications and transportation system, charging with sacredness many of its features," and just as our contemporary temples of high culture encourage development and commerce, so too did Medieval tourists encourage a proliferation of "inns, markets, and taverns."

And what treasures could be viewed! The Apostle Thomas has his finger preserved in the church of Santa Croce in Rome, this digit having once probed the side wound of incarnated God Himself. Deep within the crypt of St. Mark's Basilica, alongside the spectacularly atmospheric Grand Canal of Venice, is the mummified corpse of that church's namesake, gondolas bobbing yards away from the man who supposedly wrote the earliest of gospels. Amiens Cathedral in the town of the same name in France displays the skull of John the Baptist, now shorn of flesh, within a circular, golden reliquary that evokes the plate on which that severed appendage was brought before Herod. Not the only head displayed as a holy relic, for the brilliant Doctor of the Church Catherine of Sienna is held by the Basilica San Domenico in the community whose name she holds. That mystic, who would preach that the "path to heaven lies through heaven, and all the way to heaven is heaven," stares out from a golden box, mummified skin still clinging to her decayed face, all of which is framed perfectly by a nun's white habit. Catherine is in that category of "incorruptible saints," the holy women and men whom upon exhumation were discovered to have not decomposed, leaving behind the mummified remains that are sometimes so pristine that you can still count their eyelashes. Witness the wrinkled and grey hands of St. Zita, still clasped in repose since the thirteenth-century, or the face of St. Virginia Centurione, with her mouth agape as if she is in prayer, a pair of rosaries still being counted by her dead fingers. Even more eccentric is the Holy Prepuce, the sliver of flesh circumcised from the infant Jesus's penis, and thus after Christ's ascent into Heaven the only enduring physical manifestation of God on earth, and which appropriately looks like a wrinkled and withered flesh-colored Eucharistic wafer. A promise of the Holy Prepuce is that even after Jesus ascended, He left behind this bit of his manhood, a regenerative and procreative symbol of God's love (and of the messiah's enduring Jewishness). The only problem is that there are fully eighteen different sites which claim to be in possession of Christ's foreskin, which either implies that at least seventeen of them are fictitious, or something both prodigious and unthinkable about the Lord's manhood.

Discomfort remains for many when contemplating the dried skin and brittle bones of the saints. The Medieval trade in relics and the intricate pilgrimage routes were greatly diminished by the Protestant Reformation, but even in the earliest days of Christianity, there was an anxiety that all of this bowing and scraping before shattered bones and mummified hearts, liquifying blood and saintly breast milk, was all a bit pagan. That was the position of Vigilantius, a fifth-century Spanish Presbyter who railed against the veneration of relics, a practice already some three centuries old. Vigilantius— whose work only survives in partial quotation—was referenced by his adversary Saint Jerome as claiming that, "We are observing the introduction, under the guise of religion, of something not very different from a pagan ritual. These people can be seen kissing and adoring little piles of some kind of dust in tiny bottles, wrapped up in precious cloth." Virtually a proto-Protestant, Vigilantius similarly condemned icons, asceticism, monasticism, and saints. Jerome, the translator of the Latin Vulgate, was particularly vociferous in his attacks on Vigilantius, writing that, "We pay honor to the martyr's relics only so that we may venerate Him whose martyrs they are; we pay honor to the servants only so that the servants' honor may glorify their Lord." Ironically, pagans often noted that Christian martyrology, alongside its attendant relic veneration, was not a continuation of ancient practice, but a grotesque novelty, with the fourth-century Egyptian historian Eunapius of Sardis writing that Christians "collected the bones and skulls of criminals who had been put to death for numerous crimes ... made them out to be gods, and they became better by defiling themselves at their graves." Nevertheless, while the distinction offered by Jerome may seem purposefully obfuscating, it actually makes complete sense, despite a subtlety which Vigilantius missed. There is nothing innately holy in the bone or rag, but what's holy is that which elevates that otherwise unremarkable pile of "some kind of dust." There is a charged significance to the relic, and it's pagan largely in the enduring immanence implied by such objects, a sacralizing of material reality itself. There is, in some ways, something actually more sophisticated about this kind of worship, in my mind. A head in a box, after all, is something that you can see with your own eyes.

Among critics of relic veneration, this assumed paganism is often connected to the gory aspects of the practice, all those dried corpses propped up for view. It's true that pagans reference something very much like relics in their own writings—the bones of Orestes and Theseus were squabbled over by various city-states in the Peloponnesus, and that hades-harrowing demigod and father of poetry Orpheus's head was preserved on the isle of Lesbos where it was consulted as an oracle. The second-century Greek sophist Philostratus notes, in his *Life of Apollonius of Tyana*, that the head had floated from Thrace across the Adriatic to Lesbos, babbling prophecies all the way and treasured as an oracle by the poetic denizens of that isle, until Apollo himself arrived before the decapitated appendage and commanded it to "Cease meddling with my affairs, for I have already put up long enough with your vaticinations." The oracle of Orpheus is now apparently mute. Relics of pagans (if they were Greek and Latin speaking) and heathens (if they weren't) were often less gruesome than these previous examples, and many still survive, including such fine pieces as a sixteen-century-old oak log carved into the shape of an abstract human found in a bog near Gortnacrannagh, Ireland; a marble statue of the mystery cult divinity Glycon, the Roman snake god, discovered during the restoration of a Bucharest subway station; and arguably even the mysterious "Venus Figurines" of Neolithic Europe, presenting a zaftig woman carved in soapstone, with ample breasts, buttocks, and extended labia (whether these were mean to be fertility objects, pornography, or something else is still debated).

What must be emphasized with relics—as naturally evocative as Anthony's tongue or Catharine's head may be—is that the defining nature of such objects isn't necessarily *embodiment,* but merely *physicality.* The latter naturally encompasses the former, but nothing about the physicality or materiality of relics necessitates that such objects must be a bone inlaid with jewels, a mummified heart, a vial of a saint's tears. All that a relic requires is materiality—to be a real object in time and space of defined dimensions—as opposed to something which is abstract, transcendent, spiritual, and invisible. Relics need not be constituted of blood and tears; simply being made of atoms is good enough. And indeed, many Catholic relics are of a much less dramatic variety than a saint's tooth or a patriarch's hair but can include inanimate objects from rosaries to bibles. That is, incidentally, part of the origin of Anthony's reputation as being one who finds that which is lost, for his recovered psalter of stretched sheep-skin vellum is a relic as surely as is the saint's tongue. Anthony's psalter is particularly instructive, because it's not so different from his tongue (and both are meat, certainly): they both take part in textuality, that incarnational process whereby the divine word becomes flesh. Textuality marks the Abrahamic faiths, as different as they all are, for it's the abstraction of words, of this strange thing called language which is able to generate such things in the world, whether the logos of Christ or the initial breath of the Hebrew word

Bereshit—"In the beginning"—which manifests reality in the Book of Genesis.

Materiality and textuality are intimately connected, of course; the scroll or codex as an object—whether on papyrus, vellum, or paper—is its own type of Word made flesh. For example, there is the remarkable ancient Jewish cemetery for holy books in Egypt, the Cairo Genizah. Maintained for more than a millennium in the store-room of the Ben Ezra Synagogue in the Fustat District of Old Cairo, a congregation whose origins stretch back to the nineth-century, built and rebuilt again on the spot near where the infant Moses settled amongst the thrushes, now a handsome sand-colored building of Levantine design, all nubbled exterior and Arabesque arches, inside of which were once nearly a half million Hebrew holy texts, each tended to and venerated as if the body of a departed loved one, constituting the largest collection of Medieval works ever gathered in one place, and since dispersed among the great libraries of the world from Jerusalem to Boston, Oxford to Philadelphia, Budapest to Saint Petersburg, after Victorian classicists became aware of the Genizah's significance. For centuries the congregants of Ben Ezra kept this remarkable library safe, for as Adina Hoffman and Peter Cole write in *Sacred Trash: The Lost and Found World of the Cairo Genizah,* "these works, like people, are living things, possessing an element of the sacred about them—and therefore when they 'die,' or become worn out, they must be honored and protected from profanation." Even when a relic isn't a body, a relic is still a body. In handling the

Torah, which is after all still a physical object, in this case the scrapped, cleaned, and bleached skin of a lamb or calf, and the utmost care must be taken towards any written form of the unutterable Tetragrammaton, the four-consonant name of God. It must not be defaced or marred in anyway, but as all objects are subject to entropy, so too will there arrive a time when the Torah scroll, or some other sacred book from the Talmud to the Zohar, is no longer of any practical use.

There will come a time when the book—frayed, decaying, illegible, worn from the passing of hands—has died, and then, just as with people, they must be respectfully honored and buried. The Genizah is, in a manner, a repository of Jewish relics, textually embodied materiality as sacred as a saint's rosaries or a prophet's bone. Despite Judaism's steadfast monotheism as expressed through the formulations of the Shema, there can still be a focus on place (such as the holiness of the Temple Mount in Jerusalem) and on material objects (as with the Genizah). Both Jewish and Christian relics arguably combine a perseveration on the textual with the bodily; they each emphasize a different aspect of that pair—Judaism often associated with the textual, and Christianity with the bodily, respectively. Yet there is a bodily aspect to Judaism, the holy texts of the Genizah so tenderly cared for, and a textual aspect to Christianity's gilded bones, the latter faith seeing the incarnate body of Christ as the Word made flesh. Arguably, both were responses to a similar trauma, as the sacred space of the first-century Temple was destroyed by the Romans; that rabbinic Judaism understood the textuality of the Torah as a new site for worship, so did Christians project that sacredness onto the body of Christ (and for Medieval Christians, the body parts of His martyrs).

Today, Manseau writes, relics "have become embarrassing reminders of the dark ages of faith to many progressive believers." Our residual attraction towards relics is an attempt to rediscover something that we've lost. Both Protestantism and positivism disparaged relics as a vestige of barbarism, a superstitious idolatry, finding minor gods in a finger nail, a bit of hair, some fabric and wood. John Calvin writes in his 1543 *Treatise on Relics* that it is "impossible to have the bones of any martyr without running the risk of worshipping the bones of some thief or robber, or, it may be, the bones of a dog, or a horse, or an ass. Nor can the Virgin Mary's ring, or comb, or girdle, be venerated without the risk of venerating some part of the dress of a strumpet." (It could be countered that there is no sin in seeing the innate divinity in the bones of a donkey or the ring of a whore, but that would be a pantheism I'd imagine is beyond the numinous capabilities of the Genevan theologian.) The innate ghoulishness of these objects certainly lends itself to prurience, the stuff of eighteenth and nineteenth-century gothic novels, where the visual splendor of the Catholic Church alongside its propensity to perseverate on the bodily remains of the saints lent itself to Protestant literary agitprop. It's profoundly material—even sensual—for Catholicism was the faith of bread into body and blood from wine, of stigmatics and corporeal mortification, of beautiful Christ on the cross, and obviously of those preserved shards of humanity held in gleaming reliquaries.

Anglo-American historiography has traditionally held to certain myths, such as the belief that Medieval worshipers were credulous simpletons, and that the light of modernity and rationality during the Reformation and then the Enlightenment facilitated science, democracy, and capitalism, yet the enchantments of the relic are impossible to fully exorcize. The International Museum of the Reformation in Geneva explains in sober Swiss prose on its website that there are "authentic objects to be seen in the Museum: pictures, engravings, books, manuscripts, medals, photos, and other objects such as communion chalices, [or] watches." Not as exciting as the head of St. Catharine or the foreskin of Christ, and yet relics all the same, for presumably museumgoers would rather see Luther's own bible or the chalice of Calvin than just some old bible and chalice. Manseau writes that "the fact is that no religion, no matter how forward thinking its members consider themselves today, has been untouched by some form of relic veneration." Judaism, Catholicism, Orthodoxy, even Protestantism have their own relationship to physicality that can't but help to be expressed through relics.

Islam, as austerely a monotheistic faith as is Judaism, still countenances relic veneration, particularly among the Shia (far less so for Sunni Muslims, particularly the most fundamentalist interpretations of Wahhabism). Shia Muslims had every bit as vigorous and poetic an approach to saints and relics as did Medieval Catholicism; for three centuries starting in the sixteenth century, the Ottoman sultans collected hundreds of relics associated with the Prophet Muhammad and other Quranic figures to be housed in the Topkapi Palace, where they can still be viewed during the month of Ramadan. Here the faithful can see the staff of Moses, the sword of David, and a tooth of the Prophet, among hundreds of other relics. The Prophet's cloak is kept in a mosque in Kandahar, Afghanistan; his bowl remains in Grozny, Chechnya. Despite Islam's reputation for iconoclasm, relic veneration is as old as the Prophet, with the mystical-minded Sufi Muslims adhering to the Quranic justification that "'Surely sign of the kingship is that the coffer will come up to you ... a remnant of what" Muhmmed left behind, "the Angels carrying it. Surely in that is indeed a sign for you, in case you are believers."

Similar veneration is also common among Buddhists, particularly those of the expansive Mahayana School which plays a role within the wider faith not dissimilar to that of the Shia in Islam or Catholics in Christianity, which is to say there is a certain embrace and grounding in a physical manifestation of belief, a material, sensual, bodily understanding that is explored through relics and rites, pilgrimages and saints. Just as Muhammed's tooth is preserved in Istanbul, so is the historical Buddha Siddhartha of Gautama's incisor displayed to pilgrims in a Sri Lankan stupa, while other teeth are supposedly held in temples from Kamakura, Japan to Rosemead, California. Popular conceptions of Buddhism are of it being a body-denying faith, and yet this would be a misapprehension of the Buddha's central understanding about the omnipresence of suffering and our overcoming of that suffering. If anything, Buddhism is intimately, completely, and absolutely cognoscente of the physicality of the self, for suffering is based in that physicality. Such materiality is reflected in the popularity of relics, such as in sarira, which are small, pearl-like objects left behind after the cremation of some Bodhisattvas, Buddhist saints who are women and men that have achieved nirvana, yet choose to still be reincarnated into the indignities of life so as to help other people overcome suffering. Buddhism also has a tradition of incorruptibility just as Catholicism does, with temples from China to Japan, Vietnam to Malaysia, displaying the corpses of monks who died while meditating, supposedly able to physiologically slow their own metabolism and heart-rate until they died, leaving behind bodies that were perfectly mummified through seemingly no artificial intervention. At the Wat Khunarum Temple in Surat Thani, Thailand there is displayed the meditating body of the monk Luang Pho Daeng, in the same cross-legged lotus position he was sitting in when he died in 1973, his skin leathery and wrinkled but otherwise perfectly preserved, wearing saffron robes and a pair of black sunglasses to cover his eye sockets, apparently the only part of his body subject to decay.

Those that denigrate relic veneration as idolatry commit a category mistake; to finger rosaries before St. Anthony's tongue, to recite the Quran at the bowl of the Prophet

Muhammed, to meditate on the Buddha's tooth, is not to supplicant, genuflect, or bow down before base materiality. It's not to worship these men as gods, but rather to remind ourselves that they were men. That like you, Anthony must have bit his tongue and the Buddha must have had tooth aches. Leave the Lord to His heavenly abstractions, but relics are totems of the fallen and very understandable humanity of His most beloved prophets. Relics promise a restoration, fundamentally the same promise as genuine faith, and Julian's encomium to Saint Anthony elaborates on this detail, for the Paduan promises that "treasures lost are found again." If there is any enduring theme of the great Abrahamic faiths, it's this sense of wishing to be restored, to find what we need, to go home again. The indignity of the body is a reminder of where we're not—in heaven. Yet the body itself is an intrinsic mechanism of holiness, it is the vehicle through which we fast and feast, praise and mourn, pray and sacrifice. In that sense, criticisms such as Calvin's that we could be praying before the bones of anyone misses the point—we *should* be praying before the bones of anyone. As Peter Brown argues in *The Cult of the Saints: Its Rise and Function in Latin Christianity,* the reliquary "was a place where the normal laws of the grave were held to be suspected. In a relic, the chilling anonymity of human remains could be thought to be still heavy with the fullness of a beloved person." The anonymity is so important, because in looking at the blank eyes of a saint's skull we understand that the very point is that we could be looking at anyone—for as we are, they once were, and as they are, we shall one day be. But what makes a relic a relic is the sense of the "fullness of a beloved person," the projection of sacred meaning onto the ossuary that would be otherwise like any other.

For what the Reformation polemicists and gothic novelists got wrong was the impartation of credulity and simplemindedness unto the believer. Of course, it's a logical impossibility that all of those relics are authentic, all those multiple pieces of the true cross throughout Christendom that if assembled together would probably constitute a large enough horde that you wouldn't just be able to crucify Christ again, but indeed you'd be able to rebuild Noah's Ark too. Medieval Catholics understood this; just think of all those pilgrims in Geoffrey Chaucer's *The Canterbury Tales* making their passage through the bucolic English countryside on their way to the site of Thomas a Becket's martyrdom, who can still listen as the pardoner tells his tale of selling bags of pig bones as if they came from a saint. Chaucer writes,

By cross Saint Helen found in Holy Land,

I would I had your ballocks in my hand

Instead of relics in a reliquary;

Let's cut them off, and them I'll help you carry;

They shall be shrined within a hog's fat turd.

And yet these are women and men on a pilgrimage to *pray before relics*. Profanation shouldn't necessarily be read as being the same as lacking faith; better to see it as a paradoxical fulfillment of it. Undoubtedly many relics are genuine; *some* of those bones and bits of flesh come from the saints they're supposed to come from, but obviously many of them are inauthentic, whether from error or duplicity. Christ, after all, didn't have eighteen foreskins. And yet believers understand this, just as surely as somebody going to the Sao Paulo Museum and standing before Zurbarán's *Apparition of the Child Jesus to Saint Anthony of Padua* knows that they're looking at an illusion, a simulacra, a representation, and not an actual man. Yet it's no less beautiful despite that, just as the forged relic need not also be sacred. Just as with that glorious imitation which is art, so too do relics derive their authority by gesturing to something beyond themselves while also partaking in a presumed authenticity, even if disbelief must sometimes be suspended.

All of which reminds me of the treasures of St. Anthony's Chapel, yet another sacristy named for the Paduan, this time on the steep environs of the Troy Hill neighborhood in my hometown of Pittsburgh, only a few miles from where I grew up and still live. Home to a working-class German-American congregation founded in 1880 by a Belgian priest named Father Suitbert Mollinger, the double-steepled, tan-brick, modest chapel high upon its hill looking over the Heinz factory, the Penn Brewery, and the spires of Downtown Pittsburgh across the Allegheny River is the unlikely repository of the second largest collection of Roman Catholic relics in the world, rivaled only by the Vatican. Following Germany's anti-Catholic Kulturkampf as instituted by Otto von Bismarck, Mollinger returned to Europe to save relics from the iconoclast's hammer, enshrining them here, in Troy Hill. Within is the skull of a companion of Saint Ursula martyred alongside her, the skull of Jerusalem's fourth-century bishop St. Macharius, the skull of the fourth-century Greek dragon-slayer St. Theodore Stratelates, a complete skeleton of St. Demetrius housed beneath the altar, and a single thorn from Christ's crucifixion crown, alongside some five thousand other relics. When I first toured the chapel, which is a gorgeous, resplendent, colorful, and in the best-of-all-ways Medieval structure, the nun giving us our tour enumerated the various treasures held by St. Anthony's. Following this litany of anatomical ephemera, the sister—who was a natural performer—rhetorically asked the group "Now, I know what you're saying: how do we know that all of these relics are authentic?" She gave a dramatic pause, and with what I swear was a wink and a smile responded in her absurdly stereotypical but nonetheless charming Irish brogue, "Well, don't worry. We have papers."

Because the thing is that it *doesn't matter if those are the skulls of St. Macharisus and St. Theodore Stratelates, it doesn't matter if that's the body of St. Demetrius.* These things don't matter because they're *somebody's skulls, they're somebody's skeleton.* A relic reminds us that there is no prayer but for the tongue, there is no worship save for the knees. Relics reenchant our bodies, the physicality of the universe. They are in the purest way a living expression of the materialist's prayer. So as the faithful pray to St. Anthony to at "least restore to me peace and tranquility of mind, the loss of which has afflicted me even more than my material loss," the relic—all of those dismembered and dislocated body parts— oddly reminds us that there is nothing truly spiritually lost that is not embodied with us. The soul is a ghost of the body, a miasma of skin and bones, flesh and organs, and in our fallen, imperfect, corrupted bodies, there is beauty. Relics are merely when we recall that the body is always sacred.

Philosophically there has long been a cerebral desire to rent the mind and the body, whether in Neo-Platonism, Calvinism, Cartesianism, or scientific positivism, but the wise materialism of the relic is such that we can never forget that the thinking body is also an eating body, a sleeping body, a shitting body, a fucking body, a dying body, and a living body. Ghoulish, gothic, macabre, and morbid though something like Anthony's tongue may appear, it's also a radical invitation to embrace the canker and puss, cancer and filth, pleasure and glory, of what it means to be a human being with a body. There is no brain in a vat or a ghost in the machine, only the delightful connections of sinew to bone and organ to vein, the body in its sacred ingenuity. Praying to find that which is lost, to overcome the feeling of loss, can be compensated by the example of the relic, by the purloined body which we all possess. Rationalist attempts to drain faith of such things, of the tremendous scandal of the relic, are bound to ultimate failure for the simple fact that we can only scandalize the idea of the body itself for so long, because matter shall always have its victory. Now, contemplate that tongue of St. Anthony jetting out over a jawbone in Padua, and consider how that one lost tooth of the monk can be found in a gilded reliquary in Pittsburgh.

2 POLITICS

"*Some men look at constitutions with sanctimonious reverence and deem them like the ark of the covenant, too sacred to be touched.*"

— THOMAS JEFFERSON, LETTER TO H. THOMPKINSON (1816)

Even though his patrician family were committed Czarists and official chocolatiers to the Court of the Romanov's, Alexei Ivanovich Abrikosov rather traded away cocoa, butter, and milk in exchange for chloroform, acetic acid, and ethyl alcohol, as well as replacing his parents' royalist politics and Orthodox faith for Marxism-Leninism and dialectical materialism. As a pathologist for the Soviet Academy of Sciences, it was Abrikosov who, on the cold morning of January 23rd, 1924, first put his pale hands upon the corpse of Vladimir Ilyich Ulyanov Lenin, Chairman of the Council of People's Commissars, and the primary tactician and theorist of the Bolshevik Revolution. Within hours of his death, Lenin's corpse began to decompose, which is the fate of any organic body; his flesh cooling, rigor mortis of the muscles, autolysis giving rise to blueish blisters underneath the waxy skin of the supreme comrade. Abrikosov's task was to reverse the effects of such bloat and putrefaction, to initiate incorruptibility not through the superstitions of faith but the rigors of medicine. "All the marvels of science and the gains of culture belong to the nation as a whole," wrote Lenin in his 1918 *Third All-Russia Congress of Soviets of Workers, Soldiers, and Peasants,* "and never again will man's brain and human genius be used for oppression and exploitation." Now his corpse was to be entombed within a ziggurat of polished granite and Karelian quartzite as red as the Soviet flag, his body placed in an ornate open sarcophagus atop a basement that weighed twenty tons. Having simply embalmed Lenin, and the commissars decided that Abrikosov's job hadn't quite achieved the desired immortality, two fellow pathologists soaked the dictator's corpse in glycerol and potassium acetate. They erased blotches on his flesh with hydrogen peroxide and phenol, they pushed marbles into his eye sockets to prevent the face from collapsing. For nearly a century, Lenin has been in his Red Square repose, briefly spirited away to Siberia when the Germans invaded, and kept company from 1953 until 1961 by the corpse of his least favorite protégé Joseph Stalin before the later was reburied just outside the Kremlin's walls. Lenin's corpuscular sentry continues today, a relic of a revolution long since rolled back.

Lenin appears not as a mummy, papery and brittle, but he does look waxy. Propped up in his coffin, the father of the Russian Revolution confirms his friend Maxim Gorky's description of him as a "baldheaded, stocky, sturdy person." The ovoid head fringed with auburn hair, Comrade Lenin's neat van dyke still bristled with red, his fingers curled underneath themselves, while the left palm is flat on his black suit. Nothing about his appearance is *natural* exactly— it would be an exaggeration to say that it looks like Lenin is sleeping. The whole effect is too uncanny, too disquieting to use those kinds of terms, but despite that it must be admitted that some sort of miracle has kept Lenin's cheeks flush, his forehead unmarked, his nose from falling off. Karl Marx argued in his essay "The 18th Brumaire of Louis Bonaparte" that an authentic revolution "cannot begin with itself before it has stripped away all superstition about the past." And yet in Red Square the embalmers tended to the corpse of Lenin as if he were a pharaoh. Nor was Lenin an outlier in such treatment: for Chairman Mao Zedong lay cool in his crypt in Beijing, the body of Ernesto "Che" Guevara rests within its own Cuban mausoleum, and in the Vietnamese capital the preserved remains of Ho Chi Minh are displayed beneath a glass frame. Orthodox Marxism maintains that reality is purely materialistic, that the supernatural is merely a chimera, and a reactionary illusion at that, used to dupe the proletariat into their own oppression. Heaven was empty, God a myth, and all of religion but dangerous superstition. How, then, the decision to so manifestly display Lenin in such a way?

As the British philosopher John Gray explains in *The Immortalization Commission: Science and the Strange Quest to Cheat Death*, in the immediate aftermath of Lenin's demise, both Leon Trotsky and Nikolai Bukharin opposed such an embalming, while Stalin believed that such a preservation "would square with the Russian Orthodox belief that the bodies of saints are incorruptible and channel the religious feelings of the Russian people for the benefit of the regime." Once a candidate for seminary, Stalin intuitively understood something which his more secular adversaries couldn't grasp—that communism may claim that religion is a mere opiate for the masses, but Marxism is never more clearly a surrogate for faith than when it eliminates rival sects. As Gray argues, the "decision to embalm Lenin involved more than political calculation," for the Soviet reliquary was far from merely a cynical gambit; rather, it was a material expression of its own theological dictum. "Religion is dead," says the revolutionary, "and to honor that defeat, displayed here in this ossuary, is a relic of our saint." Incidentally, it was Abrikosov's sister Anna Abrikosova who would reject not just Marxist-Leninism, but also the Orthodoxy of both of their youths, becoming a Catholic nun of the Byzantine Rite, later dying of spinal cancer in the infirmary of the Butyrka gulag, imprisoned under orders of Stalin. Unlike Lenin, she would have no relics, for she was cremated, but despite that she remains a candidate for canonization. Persecution of individual religions is always possible, but it would seem that elimination of *Religion* itself is nonsensical. We can't help but pray to something—even when our bodies are all but burnt away, our only relics are memories of the living.

"All significant concepts of the state are secularized theological concepts" wrote the German theorist Carl Schmitt in his 1922 *Political Theology: Four Chapters on the Concept of Sovereignty,* and the immaculately preserved relics of Lenin, Mao, Ho Chi Minh don't disagree. Schmitt, incidentally, became a Nazi. Just as with communism, the religious dimension to fascism is obvious. Political and historical objects can be endowed with a charged energy, whether malevolent or not. If religious relics exist to convey holiness than political relics express power. This is something that the Allied victors in the Second World War understood well, for just as Lenin lay in repose in Red Square, so relics of Adolph Hitler could not be allowed to escape the iconoclast's hammer, lest a religious cult should grow around the dictator. And so Berlin's *Fuhrerbunker,* where in 1945 Hitler and his new bride Eva Braun each took a cyanide capsule before the Nazi leader shot himself through the side of his head, is not a place of pilgrimage for white supremacists and Neo-Nazis, because the East Germans had the good sense to pave it over and turn it into a parking lot. Furthermore, there would be no relics of Hitler, for Stalin—that man who understood the sacred import of preserved bodies so well—had the petrol-doused bones and ashes of the German leader spirited back to the Kremlin. In that place are held the worldly remnants of the man who initiated an apocalyptic war that took a hundred million lives, the incisors and canines of Hitler not in a gem-encrusted reliquary as with Anthony, but, rather, deep inside the corridors of a forensics institute. Hitler's teeth are charred black from the burning gasoline that had incinerated the rest of his corpse, some gold bridgework visible between the bones, his ironic aftermath recalling the scenes of horror from the Holocaust, where women and men had fillings pried from their mouths by concentration camp guards, where six million Jews were immolated within crematoriums. Now all that's left of Hitler remains inside of a laboratory drawer, not far from where thousands of mourners would line up to view the corpse of Lenin.

Hitler, like Stalin, understood the mysterious and mystical import of relics, the ways in which physical remnants of perceived greatness can be used to alter and shift the consciousness of a public. The Italian semiotician Umberto Eco's famous essay "Eternal Fascism: Fourteen Ways of Looking at a Blackshirt," first published in the *New York Review of Books* in 1995, observes how fascist aesthetics in general and Nazi aesthetics in particular gravitate towards an irrational syncretism, the enshrinement of a collective populace's transcendent and irrational experiences into the justification for the leader's absolute power. "The first feature of Ur-Fascism," writes Eco, "is the cult of tradition." And as cultic practice relies upon the adoration of certain objects, so too did the Nazis construct a mythos around artifacts and antiquities, remnants and relics.

The mysterious archeological activities of the Nazi Ahnenerbe Organization and Amt Rosenberg demonstrates the Third Reich's obsession with mythic justifications of their pseudo-scientific racial theories. Narratives about evil

German scholars attempting to filch the Ark of the Covenant or the Holy Grail aren't just poetic license on the part of director Steven Spielberg, but are based in the history of groups like the Ahnenerbe and Amt Rosenberg. Generously supported by the Reich, and officially connected to Berlin, the "scholars" of the Ahnenerbe and Amt Rosenberg executed archeological expeditions throughout Eurasia, as far east as Tibet, and promulgated bizarre theories regarding the supposed Aryan racial identity of Jesus Christ and the emergence of Nordic peoples from the lost continent of Atlantis. Paleolithic, Neolithic, and Bronze Age artifacts uncovered in locations in Poland, Finland, and Italy were misinterpreted as evidence of an ancient Germanic civilization. "We are the conquerors of one era and the founders of a new—also religious—epoch," wrote Alfred Rosenberg, Leader of the Foreign Policy Office of the Third Reich and patron of the Amt Rosenberg. "We bear a heavy and therefore a great destiny ... The German people is not marked by original sin, but by original nobility."

The German plundering of European art museums, where precious paintings and sculptures were often stolen by Reichstag President Herman Goering, is well-known. Less known was the establishment of a cult of Nazi relics, of ancient objects wrenched from their original context to bolster the ideological apparatus of the fascist state. At Nuremberg, where those narrow and cobble-stoned Medieval streets once hosted the quasi-pagan pageantry of Brownshirt marches (as filmed by the propaganda director

Leni Riefenstahl in her 1935 documentary *Triumph of the Will*), Hitler's government desired to create a city of relics, a veritable Nazi Vatican. There within the Katharinenkirche would be held the Imperial Crown of the Holy Roman Empire, spirited away from Hitler's native Austria following the Anschluss. Dated from the tenth century, and first forged for the coronation of the Frankish leader Otto I (though often anachronistically identified with Charlamagne), for nine centuries the crown was used during the installment ceremony for leaders of the Holy Roman Empire. Made of eight interlocking panels of hammered gold, with an arched hoop connecting front to back with the former emblazoned with a jewel-encrusted cross, the crown was intended by the Nazis to be a testament to the endurance of their supposed Reich that would last a thousand years, connecting it back to the forest primeval when Charlamagne established his dynasty in Europe. Glittering in emerald green, sapphire blue, and amethyst purple, the Imperial Crown of the Holy Roman Empire was a relic that made an argument both *spiritual* and *political*, whereby upon the collapse of the Austro-Hungarian Empire such objects "raised an outcry for union with their German fatherland," as Hitler claimed in *Mein Kampf*. Just as Christian relics connected the believer with the apostles and saints, so did such political relics connect the nationalist to their own constructed and mythologized past.

Often the religious context of such political relics was barely sublimated, as the Nazi theft of the Holy Roman Empire's imperial regalia included several important

Christian relics in addition to historical artifacts. Chief among these was the Spear of Destiny, the ostensible implement by which a centurion known as Longinus used to piece the side of the dead Christ upon the cross, showering those beneath in water and blood. Three separate claimants to the actual weapon exist; an Armenian spear, one in Rome, and the Viennese lance which was taken to Nuremberg. The occult obsessions of the Reich chancelry may have taken on a pagan gloss, yet Christian relics could play a part in the fantasies of national greatness for this Reich that was intended for a millennium but which lasted a mere twelve years. There is a twisted irony in the Nazi coveting of Christian relics, of a spear which pierced the side of a messiah declared King of the Jews. Yet their obsession was directly related to two millennia of Christian anti-Judaism, as well as the Nazi concoction of a revisionist "Aryan Christianity" which denied Jesus's Jewishness. Of particular relevance to the Spear of Destiny was the tradition which held that Longinus was of Germanic origin so that such a detail "had a unique appeal for Christians desirous of removing Judaism from the Christ story," writes Sidney Kirkpatrick in the spectacularly titled *Hitler's Holy Relics: A True Story of Nazi Plunder and the Race to Recover the Crown Jewels of the Holy Roman Empire*. According to the theorists of Aryan Christianity it was "only through struggle and bloodshed—when the Aryan Longinus was bathed in the messiah's blood—that purification and redemption could take place," explains Kirkpatrick. That the lance itself is almost certainly not the actual spear—nor are the other two candidates for that matter—is of no accounting when it concerns the dream logic of the relic. "The logical result of Fascism is the introduction of aesthetics into political life," argued the philosopher Walter Benjamin in his seminal 1935 essay "The Work of Art in the Age of Mechanical Reproduction," while claiming that Marxist states introduce politics into aesthetics. Yet arguably both of these categories—the political and the aesthetic—can be reduced to the *theological,* regardless of the relationship between them. Communists aren't scant of their own relics, as Lenin's cadaver can attest to.

Totalitarianism isn't the only political ideology which positions itself as an ersatz faith, because *all political ideologies are at their core religious.* Communism and fascism, liberalism and conservatism, socialism and anarchism, all must trade in religious vocabulary, even if secularized, for human consciousness finds meaning in things that gesture towards the transcendent, though often a meaning dimly perceived as if through a screen darkly. Because Marx was absolutely correct that we must mediate ourselves through the laws of a material world (regardless of whether or not he was correct about the supernatural one), it must be the case that certain physical objects will be charged with a superannuated significance, that even the death of God can't mean the elimination of His relics. Monarchism, justified in its decadent phase by the preposterous fiction of the divine right of kings, is the most obviously theological politics, the sovereign understood as God's physical representative on earth. It's telling that the Nazis used something as traditional as a *crown* to signal their new epoch, or that the ziggurat constructed for the leader of the Soviet regime should so closely resemble something built for an ancient Levantine king. As with anything invented by humans, monarchism's divinity is expressed through materiality, through the movement of bodies. There is the so-called "royal touch," for example, whereby it was believed that a kingly laying on of hands could cure illness, or the various resplendent dynastic accoutrements—crowns and scepters, orbs and capes—all to connect a living monarch to time immemorial. Schmitt describes how the metaphorical import of such beliefs are "transferred from theology to the theory of the state, whereby, for example, the omnipotent God became the omnipotent lawgiver," and it's difficult not to see the ways in which much of the contemporary nation—constitutions as scripture, monuments as temples, founding fathers as prophets— evidences such an argument. Which is why constitutional monarchism is so embarrassing, for the theological isn't even sublimated under the guise of secularized belief.

Historian Ernst Kantorowicz writes in his classic *The King's Two Bodies: A Study in Medieval Political Theology* that "man-made irreality … we are normally more ready to find in the religious sphere than in the allegedly sober and realistic realms of law, politics, and constitution," so that many observers can dismiss church relics as vestiges of a superstitious past, while strangely oblivious of their function in contemporary politics. For example, as with his mother, the singularly unimpressive Charles III of the United Kingdom and Other Commonwealth Realms was crowned within Westminster Abbey under the benediction of the Archbishop of Canterbury, ecclesiastical head of the Church of England of which the king is the titular head. Charles Windsor sat upon the Coronation Chair, thirteenth-century wooden furniture painted in gold and held aloft by gilded carvings of two English lions, an inset beneath the seat holding the Stone of Destiny on which Scottish chiefs were traditionally invested. The symbolism is obvious, the king crowned on both this English chair and a Scottish stone, representing his dominion over both realms. Charles was anointed with chrism poured from an eagle-shaped filigree, touched with sacred oil that connects the king back to a supposedly uninterpreted yet partially invented chronology of monarchs from the moment William the Conqueror arrived in 1066. Everything is invested with symbolic import, connotatively and denotatively connecting the monarch to political and spiritual succession, which in this case are meant to be seen as identical (the chrism, for example, directly relating to the investiture of the ancient kings of Judea, and to the Hebrew translation of "messiah" being "anointed one"). Featured on the body of Charles Windsor as he sits berobed upon the ancient, wooden Coronation Chair are the various objects that might as well be called the "relics of state," but which are technically known as the crown jewels, the regalia of monarchy.

There is St. Edwards's Crown, named after the first king of a unified Anglo-Saxon realm, and which connects the current monarch to a quasi-mythic time that precedes the Norman Conquest. Actually forged in the seventeenth-century, this crown is a baroque panoply of garnets, rubies, topazes, zircons and other precious gems, a headpiece too heavy to wear other than during the crowning itself. Then Charles held aloft various weapons with vaguely fantastic names like "The Sword of Mercy" or "The Sword of State," Renaissance forged implements of Damascus steel and Italian blade work which represents the king's role as Defender of the Faith. Particularly characteristic of the event is the Sovereign's Orb, a golden globe whose circumference is lined with jewels, atop which is a cross. To all of this finery is added a variety of robes and stoles, capes and spurs, staffs and scepters. The overall sense is, obviously, of not just profound antiquity but fabulous wealth. The overall value of the Royal Collection visited by some three million people a year at the Tower of London is officially "priceless," uninsurable against loss or damage. The antiquity and wealth of the regalia are themselves intimately related, for the first is largely fiction while the latter is undoubtedly connected to Great Britain's status as an imperial power. Very few of the objects are, relatively speaking, particularly antique, as the St. Edwards's Crown's disjunct between its name and its actual crafting can attest to. With the exception of the Coronation Spoon from which chrism is applied to the royal forehand, and which can be dated back to the twelfth-century, the preponderance of the Royal Jewels was crafted during the seventeenth-century Restoration when Charles II returned after the Republican Interregnum that began with his father's public decapitation, with the majority of the rest of the materials dating from the Victorian era.

There was a logic to concocting a fabulous and resplendent material culture connected to a supposedly unbroken chain of antiquity during Restoration, a way of Charles II emphasizing his dominion over the kingdom and the defeat of the regicidal republicans who had so recently governed. Similarly, during the Victorian Era (when the actual political power of the monarchy was quite limited), all of the scepters and crowns worn by the queen were representative not merely of that particular woman, or even of the office of the monarch, but of the temporal power of the British Empire itself. These relics of state are not just objects of monarchy, but of colonialism; far from the simple bones and rags of the saints, they are a manifestation of obscene riches, absconded from the wealth and labor of distant oppressed lands. Among the 142 objects that constitute the Royal Collection of Crown Jewels housed in the Tower of London—including sixteen trumpets, thirteen maces, seven sovereign crowns, six swords, six scepters and two orbs—is the diamond known as the Great Star of Africa (530.2 carats, largest cut gem in the world, from the Premier No. 2 mine of South Africa), the Stuart Sapphire (104 carats, from Afghanistan), and the Koh-i-Noor diamond (105 carats), once held in honor of the titular goddess of the Bhadrakali Temple in Warrangal, India and later upon the Peacock Throne of the Mughal Empire, but taken by Queen Victoria upon her acquisition of the Punjab. Saints exhibit their humanity through bone and rag; royals display their power through diamond and ruby. But as different as such materials are, they are marked by still being materials. The crystalline matrix of a diamond may organize those carbon atoms different then does a tooth, or a bit of hair, or tear of cloth, but they're still constituted by atoms, an organic bridge between the transcendent and the material.

Kantorowicz's analysis of Medieval political theology focuses on what's called the "king's two bodies," the dictum that whoever occupies a national throne is in some sense incarnating a Monarch which is eternal and far greater than whoever happens to be the ruler. Charles III may be a paunchy, 74-year-old man with a combover who stands a mere five feet ten inches tall, but as he takes up the mace of St. George, he is also that ever-living, ever-breathing, ever-ruling king that is in some far greater Kingdom than the one of mere mortals. "I know I have the body of a weak and feeble woman," Queen Elizabeth I supposedly said to her assembled courtiers awaiting the Spanish Armada at Tilbury on August 9th, 1588, "but I have the heart and stomach of a king, and of a king of England too." An apt summation of the principle of the king's two bodies, the frail physical form of whomever the individual ruler might be in hypostatic union with that divine and eternal King in the beyond. Notably, the reasoning is a closely related to the principle behind the relic, the ephemeral stuff of humanity acting as a mystery to something far greater and more sacred than our individual lives. Monarchism has always had this theme of embodiment about it, despite the apparent ethereality of the political theology which undergirds it; in fact the later depends upon the former. Think of the Protestant Elizabeth herself, who, after she died in 1603, had her bones mingled together in the ossuary with her half-sister, the Catholic monarch Mary I. This jumble of human stuff was meant to symbolize the prayer for peace of religious settlement after the brutal English Reformation. Or take the famed and ominous frontispiece of the political philosopher Thomas Hobbes's 1651 *Leviathan or the Matter, Form, and Power of a Commonwealth Ecclesiastical and Civil,* published after those hopes for religious settlement were dashed in the horror of sectarian Civil War. A potent defense of monarchism (and authoritarianism), the illustration by the French engraver Abraham Posse on the front of Hobbes's book depicts a monstrous giant who very much physically resembles the recently executed Charles I. Instead of being composed of individual body parts, this imagined king is assembled from the people he rules, so that arms and chest are made out of hundreds of small people. A state, writes Hobbes, "is but an artificial man." The ruler's organs are the ruled; the body politic is a body.

Such is the justification, through recourse to the idea of the king's two bodies, that there is *always* a monarch of the kingdom. Like dusk and dawn, one monarch perishes but the other instantly fulfills that position, despite having not yet been crowned. The eternal king's body, meanwhile, maintains its existence as it always has. This, it must be said, all seems like abject foolishness to the committed republican, and with good reason. "Mysticism, when transposed from the warm twilight of myth and fiction to the cold searchlight of fact and reason, has usually little left to recommend itself," Kantorowicz soberly intones. Yet the logic of temporal power through recourse to embodied transcendence, along with the various physical markers of that power, is hardly anathema in a democracy, especially in the permutations of that system which veer towards a type of executive Caesarism. Just as the death of a monarch means the immediate ascension of whoever is next in line, so too should it be recalled that at exactly noon on January 20th every fourth or eighth year, whoever has won the most recent electoral college vote in the United States' national election becomes the president, whether or not the Chief Justice of the Supreme Court has yet administered the oath of office. Despite having defined itself as a *Novus ordo seclorum,* a new order of the ages casting off the tyranny and imprudence of the past, the United States' executive branch bears the hallmarks of monarchical thinking, even of the king's two bodies in many ways. (The second man to occupy that position, John Adams, had wished that the honorary greeting for the president would be "Your Highness.") Think of how often people distinguish a difference between whoever of the forty-five men who've been president from that higher "Office of the Presidency," the latter apparently eternal, transcendent, and magnificent. The former can be guilty of whatever crimes men in positions of power are often guilty of, but the latter is glorious, unassailable, perfect.

Nor should it be assumed that democracy has abandoned the dream logic of the relic, for just as supposedly atheistic communism traded in the charged enchantments of the exemplary object, so too does the democratic state use a variety of material symbols of its own power which are endowed with a sacred significance, even if none of them are quite as gaudy as the Stuart Sapphire or the Koh-i-Noor. Consciously less ostentatious than a coronation, a presidential inauguration still evidences traces of its royalist roots (which is what made a committed Jacobin like Thomas Jefferson so uneasy). Consider the use of the Bible which the president is asked to place their hand upon when taking the oath of office, which is in a clear manner meant to connect whoever happens to be standing on the dais in front of the Capitol Building on a cold January morning with the long history of the Republic. George Washington's Bible, a 1767 printing of the King James Version which the first president held his hand to at his inauguration, has been subsequently used by Dwight D. Eisenhower, Jimmy Carter, and George H.W. Bush, among others. The symbolic import is clear—as all effective political symbology should be. Abraham Lincoln's Bible wouldn't be used in a presidential inauguration until Barack Obama in 2009 and then again in 2013, a former junior senator from Illinois with an intimate concern for racial justice connecting himself to the Great

Emancipator. The next time the Lincoln Bible would be used was by Donald Trump in 2017, an erasure of the singularity of the man who sat in the Oval Office before him, and who he was so clearly obsessed with. It should be noted that, true to the 45th president's reputation for frivolous grandiosity, his was one of the rare inaugurations in which he insisted on placing his hand upon *two* bibles; double the sacredness, like two divine scoops of ice cream for dessert.

Presidential ephemera has often played the role of relic in America's civil religion, a material connection to history. Washington was the exemplar of this, a man who was posed as Cincinnatus, but had a bit of the divine Augustan about him (recall, after all, that the capitol was named after him nine years before he died), an apotheosized figure in this otherwise secular nation. And the early Republic was replete with obsessive categorization of the mortal remains Washington left behind; his estate at Mount Vernon, Virginia—which is now a museum—maintains the general's Revolutionary War bedstead, his dress sword, the leather-bound, mahogany captain's chair he used as president, and his set of dentures, made not of wood as the common legend conveniently maintains, but rather teeth extracted from the mouths of the enslaved men who worked his plantation fields.

As valorized as Washington was, especially in the first half of the nineteenth century, even more of a cult would emerge around Lincoln—the United States' first martyred president—who with typological import was assassinated on Good Friday and finally expired on Easter Sunday in 1865. "When last in the dooryard lilacs bloom'd," wrote Walt Whitman of the dead president in *Drum-Taps*, "And the great star early droop'd in the western sky in the night, / I mourn'd, and yet shall return with ever-returning spring." Ford's Theater, where Lincoln was shot by a Shakespearean actor turned Confederate terrorist, maintains his box with red, white, and blue bunting, a place of national sacrifice. The chair is no longer in the theater, purchased by Henry Ford and displayed at his history museum in Dearborn, Michigan.

The Library of Congress preserves the contents of Lincoln's pockets from the day he was shot, including two pairs of eyeglasses, a pocketknife, a monogramed handkerchief, and, incongruously, five dollars in Confederate currency. And the bullet ejected from John Wilkes Boothe's revolver—having entered the skull of the president beneath his left ear, and then continued through the brain that conceived of the Gettysburg Address and the Emancipation Proclamation, the fourteenth amendment and the preservation of the Union, before fracturing the orbital plates where it was lodged—was extricated to be later displayed at the National Museum of Health and Medicine in Silver Spring, Maryland. Examined under glass, that twisted and unremarkable piece of lead looks like a slightly melted ball bearing. Mere detritus, and physically no different from any other bits of twisted metal, except this bit of twisted metal pierced the skull of America's greatest president, and so some of that sacred aura of

Lincoln is imparted to that which ended his life. Rationally, to preserve the bullet which killed Lincoln is nonsensical; it's as expendable and worthless as any other bit of grit or gravel. That such a claim is immediately suspect, that most people would of course understand why such a morbid curiosity would be saved, speaks to the enduring presence of relic logic within our culture. Theologically, this isn't transubstantiation, but the emotional register of the bullet comes from the same archetypal wisdom which sees flesh in wafer and blood in wine.

Meanwhile, the death mask of Lincoln—a common practice whereby a sculptor would apply plaster to the face of the deceased so as to make a realistic likeness of them shortly after they died—is displayed in Soldiers & Sailors Memorial Hall and Museum in Pittsburgh, only a few short miles from where you can see St. Anthony's lonely tooth. Caste on that Easter Sunday in the Peterson House where Lincoln died across the street from Ford's Theater, his death mask looks like a sculpture of a Hebrew patriarch, the president's face weary and creased, that prominent nose, those large ears, the bushel of his Old Testament beard bundled beneath his downturned neck. Displayed behind glass alongside other Civil War artifacts, Lincoln's death mask is in a building originally intended upon opening in 1910 as a meeting hall for the Pittsburgh chapter of the Grand Army of the Republic. A massive, neoclassical, Palladian structure with a tiled mansard roof, designed by architect Henry Hornbostel as an exact replica of the Mausoleum at Halicarnassus.

Sociologist Robert N. Bellah in his classic *The Broken Covenant: American Civil Religion in Time of Trial* hypothesized that the United States itself was a type of secularized religion, writing that America has "its own prophets and its own martyrs, its own sacred events and sacred places, its own solemn rituals and symbols," and of course, it could be added, its own relics. The National Mall in Washington DC, with its neoclassical edifices, was intended to appear as a New Rome, but it's just as accurate to see it as a New Jerusalem, with Capitol Hill less Capitoline than it is the Temple Mount. The museums of Washington DC are as vast reliquaries, the brutalist Smithsonian National Museum of American History not far from the red-brick castle that originally housed its treasures is as a Vatican for American civil religion, the material traces of such history imbued with a profound and charged power, housing everything from sculptor Horatio Greenough's *Washington Enthroned*, which depicted its titular subject as an Olympian god in marble, to the leather jacket of Fonzie from the sitcom *Happy Days*. According to Bellah, such places like Washington DC and its memorials are places of pilgrimage; holidays like Thanksgiving were a type of secularized ritual, the Star-Spangled Banner and the Pledge of Allegiance as liturgy, and the Declaration of Independence and the Constitution a sacred scripture.

As a creedal nation not based in common ethnicity, language, or religion, "America" itself became an object of veneration, a faith in a manner that the European powers, not founded upon an idea, never could be. The risk of a faith, however, is that it welcomes schism, and disagreement over the nature of such symbols—and relics—has generated new faiths with new creeds. Witness the US flag that was carried by insurrectionists during the January 6th, 2021 assault on the Capitol that has been used at various Republican Party rallies, notably the following year at an event held for Governor Glen Youngkin of Virginia. This flag has thirteen bars and fifty stars, but the semiotics of the relic are rather different, a direct line between this revanchist artifact and the faux crown of thorns woven by the wife of Jefferson Davis, president of the Confederate States, when he was imprisoned for sedition at Fortress Monroe. Just as Christian relics are divided from the bodies of the faithful, and from the collective body of the Church Militant, so too are the relics of democracy cleaved from the body politic. And, just as Christian relics are material manifestations of a *creedal* statement, of the Nicene and Athanasian dogmas as translated into flesh, and blood, and cloth, and bone, so too are American relics ultimately represented of something just as intangible and immaterial. Behind each American relic is that civil religion born from the Declaration of Independence and the Constitution, the former's axiom concerning "life, liberty, and the pursuit of happiness" as fundamental to this secularized faith as is the Apostle's Creed to Christianity. As for those documents themselves, the originals are held on Pennsylvania Avenue in the National Archives Building, but a few blocks from where the Capitol insurrectionists believed they were somehow saving the Constitution by overturning it. There, in a columned rotunda of the archives, surrounded by oil paintings showing various seminal historical events, and as if within the Holy of Holies, the Declaration of Independence and the Constitution are displayed in low light within sealed and temperate controlled chambers, the living creed of the American people as rendered in frayed parchment and faded ink.

3 CREATION

"Beauty always takes place in the particular."
— **ELAINE SCARRY, *ON BEAUTY AND BEING JUST***

After submerging a plastic crucifix into a jar of his own urine in 1987, Andres Serrano didn't immediately get into trouble, but it didn't take particularly long either. The resulting photograph, entitled *Piss Christ,* is a glossy Cibachrome print of five feet by forty inches; the image is of an ethereal, glowing, and golden crucifix emanating an amber shine, light seeming to propel from the nexus of the cross, the Lord sadly looking down while a line of bubbles seems to move upward towards heaven. Celestial vortices, divine eddies, and resplendent whirls, all in a glowing hue. The critic Lucy Lippard, writing in the journal *Art in America,* said that Serrano's composition is a "darkly beautiful photographic image … that is both ominous and glorious." If not for the title, it would be unlikely that a viewer would assume that this golden medium was human urine; somebody contemplating the piece might just then accurately judge it to be beautiful.

Only the knowledge of its medium is what made it an "object of censorial furor," as Lippard describes it. At the Stux Gallery on the Upper West Side, *Piss Christ* was received largely with indifference, but the reception would be far different two years later when Serrano's piece was exhibited at the Virginia Museum of Fine Art in Richmond. Because the 1989 show was in part supported by the National Endowment of the Arts, reactionaries like North Carolina Senator Jesse Helms and New York Senator Al D'Amato used the controversy as an opportunity attempt stripping that government program of federal funding.

"I am not going to call the name that he applied to this work of art," Helms pontificated, his diatribe entered into the official congressional record of May 18, 1989. "Do not dishonor our Lord," continued Helms, who in his painfully long career also opposed Civil Rights, gay rights, and reproductive rights, now deigning Serrano's photograph to be "blasphemy." This evaluation was a particularly Protestant reaction to the scandal of Christ's embodiment (though many Catholics were just as offended by the piece, obviously). Christianity generally, and Catholicism specifically, are radically concerned with materiality; with the spectacle of God made man and crucified. Because of the logic of incarnation, Christianity posits that God was a being who ate and slept, urinated and defecated. In the most sacred of ways conceivable, it is a faith of shit and piss. Boring are the heavens, but holy is the mouth and cock and vagina and asshole, the relic reminds us. As Slavoj Zizek rhetorically asks in *The Puppet and the Dwarf: The Perverse Core of Christianity*, "What if God's descent to man, far from being an act of grace toward humanity, is the only way for God to … liberate Himself from the suffocating constraints of Eternity?" There is holiness in the body, suggests such a reading, which those who venerate relics have always understood. Senator Helms's constituents may have been horrified by *Piss Christ*, but what, then, would they have made of Durbovnik Cathedral's reliquary containing the swaddling cloth of the infant Christ, a soiled diaper in Croatia a reminder that God was once man, and lived and suffered as we do?

Raised in a New York Afro-Cuban home that was staunchly Catholic, Serrano's response was perhaps as disingenuous in its surprise as it was accurate in its metaphysics, reflecting in *The Guardian* on the twenty-seventh anniversary of the NEA funding controversy that when Christ was crucified it could be expected that not only did he bleed, but he would have lost control of his bladder and bowels as well. "Maybe if *Piss Christ* upsets you," Serrano said, "it's because it gives some sense of what the crucifixion actually was like," adding that, "I was born and raised a Catholic and I've been a Christian all my life." Certainly the pious of Drubovnik, who built a massive golden reliquary furnished with arabesque angels, understood Serrano's point centuries ago. Serrano's theology—completely Orthodox, it's important to emphasize—embraces the shock of Christianity, a faith of materiality where the inglorious death of the messiah speaks to the scandal of embodiment. Christianity must be a faith of the relic, a religion that if it's true to itself cannot just be concerned with God, but also with blood, shit, piss, cum, milk, menses. Susan Signe Morrison explains in *Excrement in the Late Middle Ages: Sacred Filth and Chaucer's Fecopoetics* that there is a "profound connection between excrement, relics, and the sacred," so that "Filth is disciplined to create a space for the sacred, even becoming a sign of the sacred itself." *Piss Christ,* far from being a purposefully transgressive avant-garde (or at least not entirely those things), was in some sense a profoundly reverent work, taking Christianity on its own terms. The composition was, in its choice of subject matter and its medium, a literalization of relic logic; yet relic logic has always animated the category which we call "art," insomuch as that manner of understanding imagery and plasticity has developed out of secularized enchantments over the past four centuries.

Because in one crucially important way, Serrano's work didn't share a quality with religious relics. *Piss Christ* isn't a relic—it is a *picture* of a relic. The jar, whatever landfill in Jersey or Staten Island it now sits in, was the relic; the crucifix, wherever it was discarded, is the relic; the artist's urine, dumped in a Manhattan sink or toilet, is the relic. *Piss Christ* is simply that which is left over. This expresses a conundrum that has animated art since the advent of photography, the anxiety that silver nitrate and iodine vapor made the exemplariness of individual art works superfluous. "In all the arts there is a physical component which can no longer be considered or treated as it used to be," writes

Benjamin in "The Work of Art in the Age of Mechanical Reproduction." He argued that the process of replication—whether in photography, with prints, or with the depiction of art in books—means that aesthetics "cannot remain unaffected by our modern knowledge and power ... Neither matter nor space nor time has been what it was from time immemorial." Benjamin argues that every reproduction of an original work depletes the "aura" of that original; as an aesthetic theory, the mystical-minded philosopher tacitly acknowledges the relic logic of art itself, for just as Magritte's painting of a pipe is not a pipe, so is a poster of Van Gogh's *Starry Night* not Van Gogh's *Starry Night*. One is a relic, the other is a poster with a picture of a relic. And yet, *Piss Christ* has a sacred aura that overcomes its reproducibility, as it was still the object of defacement when a Catholic zealot attacked it while on display at a gallery in Avignon, France in 2011. Avignon, a city where the Medieval pontiff once sat upon the throne of St. Peter, and a vandal ironically turned the evidence of a relic into the relic itself.

Besides, the aura of a relic-object always had as much to say about the penitent as it did about the relic, like the dubious provenance of so many of those sacred items which still attracted worshipers fully aware of their contested lineage. Yet Benjamin's point is obviously true in its most elemental sense, and easily demonstrated by the existence of art museums, secular cathedrals that express the exact same reasoning which motivated pilgrims who travelled thousands of miles to look at the tooth of St. Anthony or the diaper of Christ. Relics can be dodgy and ambiguous, playful or mysterious, but even if there is uncertainty as to the provenance of an artifact, the logic of the object still rests on a belief in authenticity, or at least the willing suspension of disbelief. Millions of tourists a year line up to see Leonardo DaVinci's *Mona Lisa* at the Louvre rather than choosing to examine even a stunningly accurate reproduction giclée print for the simple fact that the former is *real.* That so many people pay homage to the *Mona Lisa* in person—an experience that is visually underwhelming, stressful and uncomfortable to examine a small, dark painting etherized beyond a thick plate of bullet-proof glass—rather than by simply enjoying DaVinci's proficiency with *sfumato* in a textbook, speaks to the enduring significance of a relic's aura, even, and maybe especially, with supposedly non-religious objects. Certainly it could be argued that there is a crucial variation in the quality of an experience between seeing the *Mona Lisa* in Paris and examining it as part of a slide show in an art history class, but that discounts the fact that elaborate and proficient forgeries, often perfect imitations of great masters, are instantly devalued when their duplicity is revealed. Dutch master Johannes Vermeer's *Supper at Emmaus* exuded an otherworldly charisma, which is what led to the critic Abraham Bredius referring to it as the seventeenth-century painter's unparalleled masterpiece, but in actuality it was made by the notorious hoaxer Hans van Meergeren in 1937, who was able to make sixty million dollars this way. Yet, even if *Supper at Emmaus* was the equal of Vermeer's work (it's not quite, but it's still well done), part of the power of the painterly relic is that the master Vermeer stood before that blank screen, decided how to mix green and blue and orange oil together, applied it to canvas. The actual Vermeer is understood as a relic of creation, as evidence of genius which is the currency of art as holiness is the currency of faith. In this context, a counterfeit (rightly or wrongly) is intuitively understood as something lesser.

"Genius," as an exemplary quality, is but an invention of the human imagination, the same as "holiness," but the former has a much more recent history than the latter. Few places would be more apt as the place where genius was born than Florence during the fifteenth century, when the painter, biographer, chronicler, and historian Giorgio Vasari could argue in his 1550 *The Lives of the Great Painters, Sculptors, and Architects* that "art owes its origin to Nature herself, that this beautiful creation the world supplied the first model, while the original teacher was that divine intelligence which has not only made us superior to the other animals, but like God Himself, if I may venture to say it." Thus the Renaissance, and its attendant humanism, not only saw the development of techniques, but (arguably just as importantly) developed the idea of the *artist* as a person, touched by divine gifts much as the saint was, leaving behind their works as if they were relics that mark the intersection of something transcendent within our profane world. Color and shape, linear perspective and foreshortening, the divine mimesis of the inspired soul, the process of creation itself, was now the miracle.

Simone Martini's *The Annunciation* shows a blazing field of gold behind the Virgin Mary in celestial blue, the Archangel Gabriel bewinged before her and the dove of the Holy Spirit resplendent above—the creation of incarnation. The original is at the Uffizi in Florence, and was made sometime between 1317 and 1347 for a cathedral altar in Sienna. Piero della Francesca's *The Resurrection of Christ,* the muscular Lord in red robe, haloed and triumphantly holding a martial flag while leaning upon his propped leg and starring out from the Tuscan countryside—the creation of rebirth. Original composed in 1460 and now held by the Museo Civico in Sansepolcro, Italy. *The Birth of Venus,* by Sandro Botticcello, a triumphant humanist and neo-pagan evocation of that goddess's birth from the sea foam, a luminescent vision rising from a clam shell and blown by Aurelian winds which tussle her thick, fair hair—the creation of beauty. Painted around 1480, and on display at the Uffizi. All of them attributable; no longer anonymous liturgical objects like those paintings and sculptures, mosaics and murals, icons and reliquaries of the Middle Ages, but relics testifying to the genius of the named men who created them.

All of these paintings, the originals in Tuscany, are also viewable down to the most granular detail, by the strictest parameters of verisimilitude in an Italianate building of white granite and red terra cotta roof in the middle of Pittsburgh. The Nicholas Lochoff Cloister of the Frick Fine Arts Building at the University of Pittsburgh is perhaps the single greatest assemblage of exacting replicas ever gathered anywhere, and certainly the greatest of Italian Renaissance copies. These twenty-three reproductions of Renaissance masterworks—perfectly rendered and in the exact same dimensions of the originals—were created by the self-taught savant Nicholas Lochoff. Initially a political radical exiled from Russia during the failed revolution of 1905, and a compatriot of Lenin while both lived in Switzerland, Lochoff studied and trained at being a perfect mimic of the great artists once celebrated by Vasari, with dreams of recreating a collection of these most iconic works for a post-revolutionary Moscow Museum of Fine Arts. Increasingly disillusioned with the Bolsheviks, Lochoff opted not to return to Russia after the Revolution, preferring to move to Italy where his talents were used in the restoration of original works, particularly those of the great painter Fra Angelico. Bernard Berenson, a collector who aided the university in their purchase, gathered Lochoff originals (or "originals") from Italy after the Soviet Union rebuffed Rome's offer of delivery. He had claimed that such "faithful, such scrupulous recreation by one man of the genius-born achievements of other artists had, to our knowledge … never before happened in Europe at least. Down to the minutest speck of dirt which in the course of centuries had adhered to the picture, everything was there!" Now all of these paintings, primarily visited by art history classes, ring a handsome cloister, an archive of some of the most beautiful and important paintings of the Italian Renaissance behind a granite façade that looks out upon Schenley Park and Forbes Avenue, the low rumble of busses and food carts patroned by students outside who are mostly unaware of the treasures hidden within. Endowed by Helen Clay Frick, the daughter of Gilded Age steel magnate Henry Clay Frick, the museum was able to purchase this collection at her behest in 1959, eleven years after the artist's death, for the price of $40,000.

Adjusted for inflation, and Frick's purchase would be around $385,855 today, or a little bit more than the average price of a house in Pittsburgh, and substantially less than those of some the neighborhoods closest to the museum. Meanwhile, the price of *The Annunciation*, *The Resurrection of Christ*, and of course, *The Birth of Venus*, along with nineteen other paintings in the Cloisters, is incalculable. Such patrimony is, often times, not even insurable, part of the intangible treasury of humanity, and a testament to the artistic genius of those capable of creating such works. To look upon a Lochoff is to see the deep gold of the heavenly sky in Marini's altar, the vermillion robes of Christ in the Francesca painting, the aquatic blue of Botticelli's masterwork. As an artist, he was exacting. These replicas—painted by hand just as the originals were—appear identical to those in Tuscany. If there is any difference, it's that their younger age makes them appear cleaner, fresher, more resplendent. To look at Martini, Francesca, and Botticelli is to view a painting after the degradation of five centuries of entropy; to look at a Lochoff is as if to view those originals during the Cinquecento. What, then, is the difference? Why are the originals of incalculable worth, but their perfect copies are valued at less than a third of a million dollars? Were the Uffizi to burn to the ground, we'd no doubt collectively feel a tremendous loss of our cultural inheritance; and yet the experience of seeing Christ arise from his tomb or Aphrodite carried upon gossamer waves would still be possible, at least in the Frick Fine Arts Building. The difference—obviously—is that the originals are relics of genius, of that incipient moment of creation. And the copies, no matter how glorious in their own regard, or impressive the accomplishment of he who rendered them, must remain merely second runs. Does this mean that Lochoff's immaculately executed replications are somehow not art? Any answer to a question as prosaic as that is merely an issue of philosophical discernment.

By comparison, the artifacts collected by John D. Rockefeller Jr. and displayed at the reconstructed Medieval monastery known as the Cloisters which sits at the northern tip of Manhattan in the bucolic, hilly environs of Fort Tyron Park are all entirely original. Candace Barrington, in her essay published in the anthology *The United States of Medievalism*, refers to the Cloisters and similar institutions such as Boston's Isabella Stewart Gardner Museum as examples of "tycoon medievalism," describing how both involve "self-conscious *re-creations* [that] evoke a medieval past and assert a degree of authority tied to that past through a visual culture that limns and maintains traditional boundaries." Vermillion and golden-thread Belgian tapestries from the fifteenth century; massive lead-panned German stained-glass windows of exquisite shine from the fourteenth century; a sculpture of the Virgin and her child from twelfth-century Burgundy; a carved French capital column of the distant ninth century. Naturally, there are a number of reliquaries. A silver-gilt cross crusted with gems meant to frame a small wooden shard that is supposedly a fragment of the true cross, crafted by French metalworkers more than eight hundred years ago. A massive and ornate golden reliquary shrine, long associated with a convent in Budapest but most likely assembled in fourteenth-century France, centered with an elaborate painted enamel representation of Mary and the infant Christ, the Queen of Heaven in resplendent golden robes, framed with paintings of the Annunciation and Jesus's childhood which can be folded in to close the structure, a miniature cathedral in its own right, all of it an assemblage of buttresses, ribbed vaults, and gothic arches. A stunning painted wooden bust of a woman—her identity unclear—made in the early sixteenth century somewhere in Flanders; pale skinned and innocent-smiled, thick blonde hair coiled into buns on top of her head which sits slightly at an angle, all so exquisitely crafted that it seems as if she is merely pausing in between breaths, her cheeks ever so slightly rosy. In a pendant around her neck is the relic of this anonymous saint; the name is forgotten but the flesh remains. If these were once relics, objects of devotion to the pious pilgrim, they no longer are. Now they're art.

Visitors to the Cloisters, whether they've arrived by yellow cab, M4 bus, or the A or C Train, have been encouraged to imagine themselves no longer as in New York, but rather in a gothic monastery. The materials of the Cloisters may be original, but the effect is no less a hoax than the faux-Florentine villa which houses Lochoff's forgeries. Fort Tyron Park's monastery is constructed from the ruins of actual Medieval buildings purchased by Rockefeller, disassembled, and shipped across the Atlantic. Sutured together like a taxidermized animal composed of several different specimens, the Cloisters is built from the detritus of the Benedictine Abbey of Sant Miquel de Cuixa in the Spanish Pyrenees, the Benedictine monastery of Saint-Guilhem-le-Desert in Occitan, and the Cistercian Abbaye de Bonnefont in Toulouse, the originals built respectively between the ninth and the thirteenth centuries. Attuned to the vagaries of irony and the ambiguities of simulacra, David Matthews, in *Medievalism: A Critical History*, notes how at Saint-Guilhelm's exhibition in France, "what was left in the monastery itself has been renovated … a reconstruction of parts of the cluster on the basis of work done with the materials in the Cloisters. Hence, the museum offers a very exact and very convincing facsimiles of elements of the cloister outside as it is supposed to have existed, while to see the real thing, the tourist must go to New York."

So as not to disrupt the illusion that the museumgoer has been transported to this imagined monastery which somehow exists beyond the particulars of geography and century, Rockefeller purchased hundreds of acres of the high hills in the New Jersey Palisades across the Hudson River to preserve the fantasy that this museum wasn't in the largest, busiest, and most modern city in the US, but rather in a halcyon Medieval past. The effect—as anyone who has ever visited the Cloisters, explored its rebuilt chapel or its peaceful herb garden, stood before its massive altars, or viewed its gold-topped crucifixes—is undeniably stunning. Since its walls aren't painted and plastered in white, but rather built of stone and cut with Romanesque and gothic archways, there is a convincing simulation of being in a convent or abbey, but the Cloisters is no monastery. It's a museum.

"Art for the sake of art is just another piece of deodorized dog shit," writes the novelist and post-colonial theorist Chinua Achebe in *Morning Yet on Creation Day*. Achebe was critiquing—bluntly—the Eurocentric propensity to filch objects of spiritual and political import from the Global South, and Africa in particular, and to put them in gleaming white gallery spaces with small placards next to them announcing them as "art," when their original purpose and the intent of their creators may have been very distant from that culturally specific category. Museums don't just do that with African, Asian, and Indigenous American objects—they do that with European artifacts as well, at least for the ones that were rendered before there was any belief in such a nebulous concept as art. If the entirety of the Lochoff exhibition at the Frick Fine Arts Museum can be dismissed as not being art because none of those images were original, then there is a far better case to be made that everything in the Cloisters could be considered as not art either, for the simple reason that the vast number of nameless craftsman who built these altars, crucifixes, and reliquaries had no interest or even comprehension in making something that would be comparable to a Rembrandt, a Van Gogh, a Picasso (or a Martini, Francesca, or Botticelli, for that matter). Just as "art," and especially for its own sake, is a foreign concept to much non-Western representation, so too would it have been nonsensical to Europeans in the Medieval past and earlier. The reliquary cross at the Cloisters isn't meant to be perused, but to aid in prayer; the magnificent shrine with the Virgin and Christ wasn't designed for gift-shop t-shirts and posters, but to supplicate before; the bust of the Netherlandish saint may be a curious object from an archaic past to contemporary museumgoers, but for those who made it, the piece was a living reminder of our mortality and the saving power of the Christian God. The women and men who crafted such beautiful things, mostly nameless to posterity, didn't do so as artists, but rather as pilgrims. In comparing St. Anthony's Chapel in Troy Hill, Pittsburgh to the Cloisters in Fort Tryon, New York, the objects may be physically the same, but in the first they're relics and in the second they're now reclassified as art, and that has made all the difference. Even if the Cloisters is assembled from actual pieces of Medieval buildings, and even if it's far more beautiful than St. Anthony's (which is undeniable), only the latter is still intended as a place of supplication before the sacredness of the religious relic and not just the contemplation of the artistic one.

Art has its earliest glimmerings in the Renaissance when craftsman saw fit to sign their names to pieces (at least figuratively), when Vasari could celebrate the genius of the makers as commensurate with a divine talent. By the Romantic era, a full cult of the artist took hold, replacing that of the saint, with the art piece becoming a de facto relic of secularism rather than faith. The Protestant Reformation was integral to the replacement of the relic and icon with art, and of the cathedral with the museum, but the Enlightenment is what finished this process of transformation. James Simpson writes, in *Under the Hammer: Iconoclasm in the Anglo-American Tradition*, that the "image's passage from the church to museum [was] part of the larger, violent drama of Protestant modernity and abstraction, a drama of which doctrinal positions are symptoms as much as motors of change." Simpson's argument is that the development of art as a concept necessitated a certain "image neutralization"—a discarding of the enchanted nature of materiality implicit in both icon and relic—so that objects could be viewed as neutral, disinterested, inert. The Reformation waged a violent campaign against both relic and icon, claiming that imbuing any object with a sense of the sacred was idolatry, but, as Simpson claims, the Enlightenment was able to sublimate those anxieties by inventing art as a new category. Presenting impressive inventories of Medieval Catholic artifacts purchased and displayed by English Protestant aristocrats and merchants in the eighteenth and nineteenth-centuries, Simpson makes a convincing case that the entire thinking behind "Art for art's sake," rather than relics for sacred purpose, was required by Protestant reasoning. Suddenly, looking at a reliquary in a museum wasn't idolatry, but art appreciation.

Yet the charged enchantments of relic logic weren't exorcized by art, but transformed; sacredness replaced with beauty, piety with genius. "'Beauty is Truth, Truth Beauty.'— that is all / Ye know on earth, and all ye need to know," wrote John Keats in his canonical 1819 "Ode on a Grecian Urn," a reflection on a classical vase held by the British Museum, and no doubt intended to be more functional than beautiful. Keats's celebrated lyric is so omnipresent that one is hesitant to quote it, lest an argument devolve into mere cliché; and yet even while accounting for the possibility that the poet was being ironic, the ethos as expressed in the ode is the natural result of the exact same pathos which compelled Vasari during the Renaissance. As heirs to the Romantic tradition, for good and for bad, there is a cult of art and the genius that motivates our culture, which understands the singular painting or poem, song or sculpture, as generated *sui generis* from the singular genius, the saint of the modern world whose miracle need only be originality. The Medieval craftsman who made immaculate reliquaries had no interest in originality, to "Make it new" was never their commandment, and their own brilliance (or not) was irrelevant to their task. If the Renaissance signaled anything novel, it wasn't just an advancement in certain artistic techniques, but the association of the craftsman with this new species of humanity called the artist. Reformation and Enlightenment cleaved the sacred object from its religious origin, enshrining it as art, but the cult of the genius allowed for what was effectively a new type of relic.

It's why people stand in line to see the *Mona Lisa*; it's why the Uffizi has millions of visitors to see Botticelli's *The Birth of Venus* and the Frick Fine Arts Building—holding a now technically superior painting—does not. Relic logic permeates our understanding of art; it's the need to bask within Benjamin's aura, of prostrating ourselves before authenticity, rags and bones replaced with canvas and marble. Originality wasn't a miracle to the venerators of relics, but to those who worship art—especially in our post-Romantic moment—it certainly is. That's why a Lochoff isn't regarded as the equal to a Botticelli: he was an imitator, and in the religion of art, the mere reproducer isn't a saint (or at least not until recently). Meyer Abrams explains, in *The Mirror and the Lamp: Romantic Theory and the Critical Tradition*, that for those who believed in it, the "originality of a genius is explained in large by his possessing the zeal and acuity to invent … aspects of the universe and human nature hitherto overlooked, and the imaginative ingenuity to combine and express familiar elements in new and surprising ways." It would be an error to interpret art as "secular"—because nothing is. As a category, art is strongly theological, but the saint's miracle that has been replaced is theurgical, for the artist herself now has the ability to create, as if she were God. *Materiality* remains central, whether spiritual or aesthetic. This is obvious in the hallowed sense that's imparted by those who visit our contemporary temples of art museums, the pilgrimages to the Louvre and Prado, Rijksmuseum and Uffizi, Hermitage and Met, to stand before the relics of Rembrandt and Reubens, Cassatt and Monet, Kandinsky and Pollock.

The non-plastic arts, by their nature mental and not material, have their own relic logic. Textuality by definition lends itself to an anti-materiality, but that definition has always been a superficial one. Perhaps a sonnet need only be carried in the heart, but what's to explain the obsession that compelled the stewards of the Folger Shakespeare Library in Washington DC to collect eighty-two copies of the 1623 first folio of the Bard, nearly a third of all of those printings in existence? The scholarly import of examining those volumes isn't non-existent, but it'd be disingenuous not to acknowledge the fetish quality here, the way in which though its contents are identical to anything you can find on the shelves of a local library or a suburban strip mall Barnes & Noble, this four-hundred-year-old printing is still understood as a conduit to Shakespeare. That Bardolatry emerged in Protestant England, an answer to the stripping of the altars and the demise of relic veneration, is not incidental.

Or, consider the strange melancholy of writer's museums, ever popular in the United States, where some compulsion convinces readers that they can better understand Walt Whitman by going to Camden or Emily Dickinson by traveling to Amherst rather than by reading *Leaves of Grass* or the *Collected Poems*. "How a house is lived in can tell you everything you need to know about people," writes Hermione

Lee in the preface to *Lives of Houses,* "whether it's the choice of wallpaper, the mess in the kitchen, the silence or shouting over meals, doors left open or closed, a fire burning in the hearth." She's correct, of course. In going to that Amherst attic and viewing Dickinson's floral wallpaper, that shining white dress hemmed for such small stature, and the scraps of envelope on which her prophetic verse was written, to see the whisps of auburn hair preserved as if from a saint, the reader can absolutely better understand "Because I could not stop for death." They can intuit such verse by seeing the anchorite's cell where it was imparted.

There is always an opportunity for iconoclasts. The twentieth-century avant-garde, including Dadaism and conceptual art, challenged the cult of genius and the object as relic, though Marcel Duchamp's still-shocking signed urinal now exhibited in the Museum of Modern Art perhaps affirms the importance of materiality as much as it denies it. Our great theorist of artistic mechanical reproduction was Andy Warhol, who both challenged the cult of genius but also embraced a quasi-Medieval understanding of the relic, his celebrity paintings appearing nothing so much like the icons he would have viewed as the son of Ruthenian immigrants who grew up across the valley from where one day the Frick Fine Arts Building would stand, and who prayed in the Byzantine Rite St. John Chrysostom Church in Pittsburgh. Yet, despite his assembly line production of art pieces, his own sometime limited role in the execution of individual works, and his valorization of reproducibility, Warhol was nothing if not a lover of materiality, with a Catholic's sense of the sacredness of the physical object itself. Brillo Boxes and Campbell's Soup cans, Coke bottles and Hollywood magazines—none of them may be singular, by their very nature, but they're nothing if not intimately and gloriously physical. They have texture, heft, dimension.

Relics always exist within the tension of veneration and degradation, the iconoclast's hammer competing with the pilgrim's knee. Contemporary art both denies and embraces the relic logic which is implicit in the supposedly-secular category of art anyhow. It's fascinating to imagine what Warhol would have thought about digital art, particularly in its most recent iteration of non-fungible tokens, or NFTs. A unique digital identifier based on computerized blockchains, NFTs have been used in the production of art which exists in no physical space, but that preserves the concept of it being a singular piece, which can be possessed by a specific owner. Benjamin asked how art would be effected by the reproduction of a million copies of a painting; the NFT envisions a seemingly infinite number of digital copies, but only one which is "real," or only one person who "possesses" it (even though we can cut-and-paste the image and save it as a JPEG to our own computers). In 2022, a crypto-currency trader named Martin Mobarek, in an act far more blasphemous than anything which Serrano did, apparently destroyed an original Frida Kahlo drawing after converting it into an NFT which he possessed. "I own the painting," Mobarek told reporters, "by burning it, I am immortalizing it." The ultimate victory of the Platonist, the Cartesian, the iconoclast; a veneration of the invisible spirit over the tangible body, a dismissal of the physical in favor of the purely idealist. Yet the dealer emphasizes that he possesses the NFT, and so originality, authenticity, singularity, are ever victorious. The relic is not abolished—it is merely uploaded.

4 FAME

"I think that when you are famous every weakness is exaggerated ... Goethe said, 'Talent is developed in privacy,' you know? And it's really true ... Creativity has got to start with humanity and when you're a human being, you feel, you suffer. You're gay, you're sick, you're nervous or whatever."

— MARILYN MONROE, *LIFE MAGAZINE*

So water-logged and bloated was the bruised and empurpled corpse of Percy Bysshe Shelley that when the dusk tide of the Bay of Naples washed his drowned remains into the sands of the Viareggio coast, it was only a copy of John Keats's vampiric poem *Lamia* in the breast pocket of his jacket which announced his identity. For four days after the ship *Don Juan* and all four men aboard went missing, his wife Mary and friend Lord Byron could hope that Shelley had somehow survived, but the grim remains on the Italian beach dissuaded any of that possibility. The brain that had formed the lines "Nothing beside remains. Round the decay / Of that colossal Wreck / boundless and bare" had his flesh devoured by kingfish and snook, snapper and redfish, leaving behind only a damp assemblage of parts that had once been a poet. Only 29 at the time of his tragic death in 1822, and where perhaps earlier poets had believed that a lifetime of experience was necessary to render the greatest of works, the Romantic generation had assented to a cult of youth. And, where past authors had disappeared into their verse, more functionary bureaucrats of inspiration than ecstatics themselves, the Romantic sensibility valorized the all-seeing, divine "I," the sense that the narrator of a lyric was the writer, and that all true art was, in the words of William Wordsworth, "the spontaneous overflow of powerful feelings."

Neither a trade nor a hobby, the Romantic saw poetry as vocation, as a means of transforming their souls. They were, at the risk of courting the glib, the first rock stars. After all, part of Shelley's legend was his young death, and it must be noted that he only lived an extra twenty-four months compared to Jim Morrison, Jimi Hendrix, Janis Joplin, Brian Jones, Kurt Cobain, and Amy Winehouse. As with the rock stars of a century-and-a-half later, this was the coterie of youthful, beautiful, and scandalous artists whom could be described as "mad, bad, and dangerous to know," as in the words of Lady Caroline Lamb about her lover Byron, he and his friends widely understood as radicals committed to individualism, to excess, to revolution (literary, if not literal). "I know the precise worth of popular applause," Byron wrote to his publisher John Murray, "for few scribblers have had more of it." Byron, fantastically handsome, ridiculously wealthy, appropriately scandalous, was very much a celebrity at the dawn of that concept, his name and image known from the Halls of Westminster to which inheritance entitled him privilege, to the islands of the Peloponnese where he would aid the Greeks in their war for independence. Looking a bit like the silent film star Rudolph Valentino, Byron was merely the nucleus of celebrities, famous not just for their talent but tautologically for being famous. As Byron wrote to Murray, in language prescient of Hollywood tabloid columns, the poet understood himself to be a "popular idol." Before the Romantics it would have scarcely occurred to readers to care about the personal life of those who created the art we consume (hence the boring, suburban life of William Shakespeare later engendering so many preposterous conspiracy theories about his authorship). Theirs was a cult of genius, but genius as it inevitably transitions into its more democratic partner of fame.

Fred Inglis, in *A Short History of Celebrity,* the cover of which features Byron superimposed over Marilyn Monroe, notes that fame, as incubated during the late eighteenth and early nineteenth century, involved "new doctrines of the feelings … [a] conjunction of aesthetics and ethics, their radical displacement of the stolid cardinal virtues, temperance, justice, fortitude, by such fiercer-burning and colorful passions and qualities as desire, spontaneity, abandon, ardor, eagerness." To live such a life is always to risk the power of the divine, to find oneself beset by the demons of opium addiction like Thomas De Quincy and Samuel Taylor Coleridge, to leave a beautiful tubercular corpse like John Keats or a prematurely decomposed one like Shelley. Despite his youth, or perhaps because of it, there was a reverence paid to the tragic poet, and to the inert mass of his body brought in with the tide. A pyre was built upon the coast, and all that was left of the genius was immolated in the Mediterranean sunset. Byron left the service early, and Shelley's brilliant wife Mary, whose *Frankenstein* is the greatest literary work about the *elan Vitale* of materiality, wasn't even present. A mourner, most likely the now-forgotten novelist Edward Trelawny, supposedly thrust his hand into the burning mass and retrieved from the flaming corpse of Shelley his preserved heart, so perfect that not even fire could touch it. Trelawney would latter mummify the heart in a cask of wine and spices, not quite incorruptible, but close enough. Since the preservation of that relic, the organ has been reburied with the rest of Shelley at the Protestant Cemetery in Rome, but some pathologists have conjectured that the heart's resistance to flammability was less because of divine genius and more the calcification engendered from a previous tubercular infection. Still others maintain that it wasn't his heart at all, but actually his tough, sinewy, scarred cirrhotic liver, impervious to the damage of the flames.

From the Medieval cult of piety came the Renaissance cult of genius came the Romantic cult of celebrity, but the thorough line remained the object, the way in which a material marker can connect the supplicant to things which are greater than themselves, whether a saint's shinbone or a movie star's autograph. The Romantic era saw no shortage of material effects generated from the lives of its famous poets, artifacts of celebrity as surely as the tooth of St. Anthony or the head of St. Catharine of Sienna were material testaments to their holiness. Deborah Lutz notes, in *Relics of Death in Victorian Literature and Culture,* that "Little pieces of the bodies of the Romantic poets and their friends and lovers can be found, today, scattered about the world in archives, libraries, and museums," describing her own handling at the New York Public Library of fragments of Shelley's skull that "appear like sections of veined, dried leaves, with a russet color and shaved so thin they are almost transparent." The Keats-Shelley House in Rome lists on its website a number of relics (that is the word they use), including Keats's death mask, locks of hair from the museum's two namesakes, a dagger from Trelawny (perhaps that's what he used to pry that heart/liver loose?), and an urn with a small portion of Shelley's jawbone. Reflecting on such ghoulish ephemera, Lutz says that those who handle these objects are overcome with questions, such as, "what meaning comes embedded in the corporeal trace? Why would such a grisly reminder of annihilation, of a body lost forever, be cherished, kept, shown about?" Relics from Padua to Pittsburgh, Rome to Cleveland's Rock and Roll Hall of Fame, raise such questions; the Romantics neither posed new questions nor answered, they merely broadened the kinds of bodies that such artifacts could be pulled from. Ironically, one thing which the saint and the celebrity shared, was the virtues of suffering and the validation of sacrifice, whether a martyr or a rockstar member of the 27 Club.

Fame isn't a Romantic innovation, even though celebrity very much is. The saints, after all, were famous. At a baseline level fame simply means that more people know who you are than you happen to know people in return. There had, of course, been famous poets and athletes, musicians and artists, into dim antiquity. Celebrity is a bit different, the valorization of fame itself, and in direct lineage from the Medieval enshrinement of holiness. If genius still had theological associations about it, a sense of the divine touch, then celebrity was wholly more secularized, a sense in which both the individual talent and the fans who return the superstar's love are justification enough. There were precursors obviously; Leonidas of Rhodes, Milo of Croton, and Chionis of Sparta were all celebrated athletes, respectively in running, wrestling, and jumping; Antigenides of Thebes was a great flautist, Herodorus of Megara known for his skill on the salpinx, and Terpander beloved for his voice; Praxiteles is remembered for his sculptures even today, as Cimon of Cleone is honored for his painting. They prefigured the cult of genius which Renaissance artists tried to emulate, but celebrities are a more modern creature. As early as the Italian poet Petrarch there may have been a gesture towards celebrity as we'd understand it today, a desire in his fourteenth-century *Il Canzoniere* for that which "makes men immortal through fame," without recourse to the piety of the saint. Still, nobody could accuse Petrarch of not being a figure who perseverated on (and was indeed possessed by) genius. Yet by the nineteenth century, genius had metastasized into celebrity, and it appeared in a manner that is still familiar to us almost two centuries later. Consider youths seduced into suicide by Goethe's *The Sorrows of Young Werther* as surely as concerned parents claim heavy metal lyrics have driven their teenage sons mad; a type of nascent Beatlemania accrued around figures as varied as Ludwig van Beethoven and Charles Dickens, Giuseppe Verdi and Charles Baudelaire. These figures, argues Inglis, "announced a new bill of rights to feelings, in which art figured largely as both vehicle and tutor of those feelings." Just as the saint enshrined certain communal Christian values, so the celebrity was a conduit for individualist virtues. "The artist," writes Inglis, "leads the way to the wonderful land where the new man and the new woman will come to realize in a perfect equality of being all that they might become if only the everyday world were not too much with and for them." Celebrities—they may be more popular than Jesus, but they're also just like us.

From Shelley's heart in a jar to photos from *Vogue* taped on a teen's wall like icons in an anchorite's cell, celebrity was conceived in the nineteenth century and birthed in the twentieth. This "Romantic cult of genius that ushered in the 19th century led to the fin de siècle worship of personality," writes Sharon Marcus in *The Drama of Celebrity*, when the "modern meanings of the word 'celebrity' and 'star' first became widespread." There is a metaphorical transference in interpreting the physical remnants of Shelley as being "like" a relic, but the phenomenon of visiting his regathered fleshy portion in the utilitarian Protestant Cemetery is identical to visiting the mausoleums of Valentino, Douglas Fairbanks, Jayne Mansfield, or Judy Garland at the Hollywood Forever Cemetery off of Santa Monica Boulevard, or going to Paris's famed Pere-Lachaise to genuflect before the earthly remains of Sarah Bernhardt or Oscar Wilde, both instrumental in creating the image of the modern celebrity. That same cemetery entombs Jim Morrison, two years younger than Shelley when he died, and who, for what he lacked in the latter's lyrical genius, makes up for it in the enthusiasm of his contemporary fans, who five decades after his accidental drowning (albeit in a bathtub while he was overdosing on a highball) still visit the graffiti-bedecked memorial featuring a handmade bust of the rock star left by a fan. Mr. Mojo Rising, the Lizard King, an American poet, he of the dorm room poster featuring the shirtless Morrison with tussled hair and beaded necklace, treated with the same reverence of relic logic. Not that Morrison is exemplary in this regard; rock and roll produced superstars, its own saints with their own liturgy, their own pilgrimage routes, and their own relics, from the moment the genre became a cultural force. David Shumway writes, in *Rock Star: The Making of Musical Icons from Elvis to Springsteen*, that the "force of stardom helps explain rock's cultural reach." Unlike early genres, where performers and composers could be lauded, even for genius sometimes, rock stars elevated the genre into the quasi-theological, and a certain enchantment of materiality followed.

"All stars are celebrities," writes Shumway, "but not all celebrities are stars." This is a crucial difference, and it explains how fame changed in the nineteenth and especially the twentieth century, where the enchanted aura which surrounded certain figures elevated them to cultural sainthood. Shumway considers James Brown, Bob Dylan, the Rolling Stones, the Grateful Dead, Joni Mitchell, Bruce Springsteen, and of course Elvis Presley (the last of whom has actually had a religion develop about him). To that list could be added a whole litany of rock stars; Lou Reed and David Bowie, Marvin Gaye and Bob Marley, Prince and Madonna. The Beatles. The formalist fantasy of being able to separate the text seamlessly from its creator is made null by the example of rock stardom, as foolish as separating the saint from their miracle. And this divination of rock stardom would manifest in recognizably religious forms, from the exegetical debates about Dylan lyrics to the bootleg Grateful Dead recordings shared as if epistolary manuscripts amongst the early Christians. "Loving classic rock has always been an act of faith" writes Stephen Hyden in *Twilight of the Gods: A Journey to the End of Classic Rock*; "albums as sacred texts, live concerts as quasireligious rituals, and rock mythology as a means of self-discovery." Notably for all of these rock stars is their canonization within an official list as having ascended to the Rock and Roll Hall of Fame. This institution is many things—a tourist attraction, a marketing opportunity, a gimmick, and a shrine.

To be clear, what the Hall of Fame is after is something grander than simply compiling a canon, a playlist, or a mixtape. The name of the institution calls to mind not the required listening section of a college music appreciation class syllabus, but rather Elysium or Valhalla. Not for fans, but pilgrims. Often the focus of mocking condescension from listeners who nonetheless debate the merits of who has been included and those who've been excluded, a visit to that Cleveland institution demonstrates the endurance of relic logic. A modernist pyramid designed by architect I.M. Pei, when approached on a cold, Cleveland morning appears imposing, reflected in the frozen, cracked surface of Lake Erie and underneath gray overcast Ohio skies. Within the massive edifice—which very self-consciously presents itself as a shrine—the supplicant will find an assortment of material objects which are notable only by their one-time proximity to the honored saints. Music is mediated through either records or live performance, but the pilgrim to Lake Erie can also approach these saints through relics like Elvis's black jumpsuit, Dylan's harmonica, Johnny Cash's 1943 Martin Guitar, Sid Vicious's sleeveless t-shirt, Ian Curtis's handwritten notes to "Love Will Tear Us Apart." In the most obvious way, listening to the '68 *Comeback Special*, *Blood on the Tracks*, *At Folsom Prison*, *Never Mind the Bollocks*, and *Closer* will tell you more about Elvis, Dylan, Cash, the Sex Pistols, and Joy Division than seeing some clothes, a rusty harmonica, an old guitar, a t-shirt, and some napkin notes will—but at the level of faith, don't discount their power. When the Rock and Roll Hall of Fame mounted a 2000 special exhibition entitled *Lennon: His Life and Works*, visitors to the gallery first saw his silver, circular, wire-frame glasses, cracked and covered in his blood, as if just picked up from the pavement in front of the Dakota. As clear a relic of a martyr as can be imagined.

Halls of Fame—from Detroit's Automotive Hall of Fame to the American Theater Hall of Fame in New York, the Poker Hall of Fame in Las Vegas to the Hall of Great Westerners in Oklahoma City, and a hundred other examples dedicated to everything from gospel music to bowling—can trace their origins to the same Romantic nationalism from which the concept of celebrity itself developed. Eveline Bouwers notes, in *Public Pantheons in Revolutionary Europe: Comparing Cultures of Remembrance, c. 1780-1840*, that with the "devaluation of Church power, the established canon of saints increasingly faced competition," so that "Across Europe … a literary cult of great men emerged that rivalled with conventional … myth making." Representative would be the Pantheon in Paris, a secular temple inaugurated by the inheritors of the Revolution, and dedicated to the great men (and later, women) of the Republic, particularly Voltaire and Jean-Jacques Rousseau, the second of whom was disinterred and brought back to the capital for state honors while the guillotine was still set above the Place de La Concordia, and the relics of the Roman Catholic Church were being smashed in the streets and alleys. One cult of saints may have been in eclipse, but another based in fame was only just being established. It wouldn't be limited to France either, with representative examples throughout the continent. These institutions were marked by a "hazardous union of secular and sacral cultures of veneration," explains Bouwers, where temples disenchanted of traditional religion "would be supplanted by the cult of the fatherland and the tomb of a hero would become an 'altar of liberty,'" or now, as the case may be, an altar of rock music, football, rodeo cowboys, or bowling.

Stern and austere, the neoclassical edifice of the Walhalla Memorial has loomed over the Danube River since it opened its columned portico to visitors in 1842, conceived by the Crown Prince Ludwig of Bavaria as a granitoid argument for German unification. An architecturally histrionic celebration of all things Teutonic, Walhalla displays over a hundred busts of figures over a two millennium period, include Goths and Vandals, Lombards and Swabians, Angles and Saxons, Bavarians, Prussians, Austrians, Swiss, Swedes, and German speakers in Poland and Russia. Gazing out from vacant marble eyes are busts of King Otto I of the Holy Roman Empire and the Hapsburg King Charles V; scientists like Copernicus and Gregor Mendel; writers from Erasmus of Rotterdam to Goethe; musicians such as Wolfgang Amadeus Mozart and Beethoven; even reformers like Martin Luther, who thought they'd done away with pilgrimages. Following Germany's defeat in the Second World War, several more busts were added, including such figures as Albert Einstein and the resistance fighter Sophie Scholl. Inaugurated by

Ludwig, maintained under Bismarck, the Kaiser, and Hitler, redefined in West Germany and now again in a reunited nation, Walhalla has meant variable things depending on the government that pays to keep it clean. But the name of the building itself, with its reference to the astral Norse domain of the fallen great, inevitably conflates fame with the sacred, regardless of whether the site is run by royalists, fascists, or democrats. Nor was the Walhalla the only such site conceived of by Ludwig, for only fifteen years later he'd lay the cornerstone for another edifice, the Doric colonnaded Ruhmeshalle near Munich—the first such structure whose name literally translates to "Hall of Fame."

From Munich then, there is a direct line to Cleveland. Ruhmeshalle is the most clearly stated temple to fame, and the predecessor of not just the shrine to rock music in Cleveland, but also Cooperstown, New York with its National Baseball Hall of Fame, the Hockey Hall of Fame in Toronto, or the Pro Football Hall of Fame in Canton, Ohio. The severe Greco-Roman intimidation of Walhalla and the Ruhmeshalle may seem distant from the circular, concrete bungalow with a football-shaped dome in Canton, but the relic logic that motivates both sites is clear. If anything, the presence of not just busts and plaques, but of the actual material accoutrement of the men it honors, makes Canton, Cooperstown, and Toronto more similar to Medieval reliquaries than the Ruhmeshalle is, even if the Pro Football Hall of Fame only contains jerseys and balls handled by Johnny Unitas, Joe Montana, and Dan Marino (not their jaw bones and ribs). Athletics arguably gives an example of the most venerable form of secular fame, the objectivity of evaluating physical prowess, placing Leonides of Rhodes, Milo of Croton, and Chionis of Sparta with Babe Ruth, Tom Brady, Michael Jordan, Wayne Gretzky, Muhammed Ali, and Pele into the same category.

Sports, furthermore, especially with the quasi-pagan valorization of physical strength and beauty, has always had about it the glow of enchantment. To run faster, jump higher, hit harder contains qualities of wonder and amazement, which is to also say the transcendent and the numinous. Rebecca Alpert writes, in *Religion and Sports: An Introduction and Case Study*, that "the fallible hero who makes good, the ritual celebrations, the connection to a historical tradition, the meticulous keeping of records, the loyalty of fans across generations, and the sense of a cosmic connection to something outside oneself—all are markers of religious experience as it is commonly understood."

Added to that could be the *materiality* of both practices, for athletics are so obviously physical that it can't help but generate relics, and it often labors with a similar sense of martyrdom. Examine the bruised, battered, and busted face of boxer Jack LaMotta, suffering for his vocation like Sebastian buffeted by a dozen arrows. Sports aren't just defined by physicality, but like religion there is a Platonism involved in the activity, and, maybe even more crucially, in the viewing of it. Watching Ted Williams hit his final Fenway homerun at the bottom of the eighth in 1960, with the Red

Sox down 4-2 against the Orioles, novelist John Updike noted in *The New Yorker* (no doubt to the chagrin of many Yankees fans) that "It was in the books while it was in the sky," the parabola of a ball soaring over the Green Monster now apotheosized, not in the realm of physics so much as metaphysics. Now in Cooperstown you can see the camera which captured that moment, alongside any number of important balls. The reality is that a visit to any sports Hall of Fame is, in a literal sense, not much different than going to Dick's Sporting Goods. A football is a football is a football. Except it's not, of course, at least not if we're privy to a sense of the holy. For a regular football may look indistinguishable from that identical object which was used in the final play of the 1973 AFC Divisional Game between the Oakland Raiders and the Pittsburgh Steelers, but a visit to the Western Pennsylvania Sports Museum illustrates the aura of the relic. This, within its glass case is no ordinary football; this is the object grasped from gridiron oblivion a mere inch from the AstroTurf by fullback saint Franco Harris and propelled into the endzone for the Steeler's winning touchdown in the final seconds of a game they'd been losing. An immaculate reception, as sportscaster Myron Cope waggishly but perceptively called it.

We've always had athletes, but the twentieth century saw an entirely novel form of fame with movie stars, a variety of celebrity contingent upon modern technology to give it its power and aura. True that theatrical performance has as long a history as sports or music, and that there was no shortage of celebrated actors in the centuries before film's invention. The Renaissance had its Ned Alleyn and Will Kempe, the Restoration had Elizabeth Barry, Thomas Betterton, and Nell Gwynne, the nineteenth-century Edwin Forrest, William Charles Macready, Edwin Boothe, Ira Aldridge, and Sarah Bernhardt—but we've got no *recordings* of them. They were performers, famous, maybe even celebrities, but they're not stars. Rather, stardom is mediated through the black-and-white silent majesty of Valentino and Douglas Fairbanks; the jester's antics of Charlie Chaplin and Buster Keaton; the regal forbearance of Clark Gable; the sultry humor of Mae West; the physical pyrotechnics of Fred Astaire, Ginger Rogers, or Gene Kelly; the rumpled cool of Humphrey Bogart; the throaty elegance of Marlene Dietrich; the Atlantic sophistication of Cary Grant and Joan Crawford; the stolid conservatism of John Wayne; the small-town charm of Jimmy Stewart; the rock-jawed masculinity of Kirk Douglass; the sex appeal of Rita Hayworth; the wounded innocence of Judy Garland; the icy beauty of Grace Kelley; the rebelliousness of Marlon Brando, Steve McQueen, and James Dean; the Hollywood reinventions of Paul Newman, Robert DeNiro, Dustin Hoffman, Al Pacino, Meryl Streep, Anjelica Huston, Robert Redford. *They* are stars. Who the hell are Ned Alleyn and Edwin Booth? Footnotes in a theater history monograph.

Hollywood, from the earliest days of silent film, has been deeply invested in celebrity. Some are stolidly consistent—Cary Grant is always witty and sophisticated, Harrison Ford always gruff and smart-assed. There are actors who are forever variable, the Stanislavsky Method athletes from Brando to Daniel Day Lewis. But whatever the type of Hollywood actor, the idea of being a *star* fundamentally marks such actors as a new type of human. There's a phenomenological difference in seeing women and men elevated to multistory celluloid, for their speech and appearance, carriage and intonation, to be affixed permanently in film. Immortality may be an illusion, as enduring as the film strip (and many of the earliest are already a pulpy mass of flammable acid), but it's a powerful illusion nonetheless. Jeannine Bassinger writes in *The Star Machine* that "Hollywood would have loved to ignore the fact that movie stars were human beings," but that the studios inevitably had to deal with their celebrities "personal situations, things that couldn't be predicted or controlled: anger, breakdown, failure, bad behavior, and disappointment." This, I would argue, is only partially accurate, for while I'm sure that Metro-Goldwyn-Mayer, Warner Brothers, and Paramount would have preferred that personal tragedies not economically threaten production, the reality is that from a publicity standpoint, audiences thrill to the agony and ecstasy of movie stars. Celluloid transubstantiated them into stars, but as saints requite a certain amount of suffering, audiences are naturally drawn to misfortunes of brilliant performers. Handsome and taciturn James Dean and his Porsche 550 Spyder on California Route 46, absurdly beautiful Marilyn Monroe with her emptied bottle of pills, glamorous Sharon Tate and her nightmarish death—they almost recall a Medieval martyrdom.

Stars, like saints, clearly leave their own relics. Just like every other form of celebrity, there are the remnants of materiality which gesture towards divination. Celebrity relics derive value from their one-time proximity to those who are famous, immeasurably more important a quality than if they're made of expensive materials or expertly crafted. Audrey Hepburn's black dress from *Breakfast at Tiffany's* is undeniably chic, but it's the fact that it once hung from her slender shoulders that made it worth $920,000 in an auction at Christie's. Producer David O. Selznick's Best Picture Oscar for *Gone with the Wind* appears identical to every other gold-tinged statue that an awardee has received, but it was his Academy Award that sold for one-and-a-half-million dollars, purchased by another star, the "King of Pop" Michael Jackson in 1999. The piano on which Bogart and Ingrid Bergman where serenaded by Dooley Wilson's rendition of "As Time Goes By" in *Casablanca* sold in 2014 for a little over three million dollars, despite missing several keys. The entirety of actress Debbie Reynolds's Hollywood memorabilia collection is valued at twenty-five million dollars.

Then there are those celebrity relics which are maintained by public collections. The Museum of Natural History in Los Angeles contains a large assemblage, including Scarlet O'Hara's dress worn by Vivien Leigh in *Gone with the Wind* and Chaplin's "Little Tramp" costume. Meanwhile, the Smithsonian Museum of American History, arguably the

United States's surrogate for the Pantheon or Walhalla, exhibits an assortment of celebrity relics, most famously the ruby red slippers worn by Dorothy as portrayed by Judy Garland in *The Wizard of Oz,* among the most visited displays in the museum.

"It wasn't a dream, it was a place," Dorothy tells her family after she has returned to Kansas from Oz, and the Hollywood relic would seem to be proof that the technicolor fantasies of film are in some material sense real. Despite Monroe's otherworldly beauty, we can see evidence of her existence in the form of her white dress from *The Seven Year Itch;* regardless of James Dean's alien coolness, that he was once a living man, an actor with a job, is proof enough in his leather jacket from *Rebel Without a Cause.* What gives relics such power is this formula—that they connect something which is greater than prosaic life to a simple object. It's not that relics betray those who once possessed such things (whether the tooth of a saint or the dress of a movie star) as being mere people, but that they remind us of the divinity implicit within all humanity, of the potential for greatness that we can share in. There are no relics of God the Father, for He is without form, but there are millions for His saints, His artists, His rock and movie stars, and they exist as both example and promise. A religion of pure spirit is as good as no religion at all, for the impulse to make faith only of heaven is to exorcize the world of its soul. Crucially, the relic is a reminder that real people were capable of such things.

Disturbing, then, to consider that a hologram provides not a trace of a relic. We're now at a technological cusp where artificial intelligence and deepfakes will fulfill the studio desire of film without the messiness of human stars; where faces and voices with no interiority, no consciousness, no mind or soul will be capable of imitating anyone, not least of whom the pantheon of movie stars come and gone. When a 2005 Volkswagen commercial featured a computer altered clip of Gene Kelly popping, locking, and moonwalking to a techno version of the titular track from *Singing in the Rain,* it looked janky and awkward. Methodology has improved. Soon, digital resurrection will be possible, celebrity born not from flesh and blood but from algorithm, a far more fake type of silicon enhancement than is normally the case in Los Angeles. "Simulation is no longer that of ... a referential being or substance," wrote the French philosopher Jean Baudrillard in his 1981 *Simulacra and Simulation.* "It is a generation by models of a real without origin or reality." With deepfakes, perhaps you'll one day seamlessly see Robert Redford in *The Godfather* or Sean Connery in *Lord of the Rings.* Maybe you'll see Marilyn Monroe, Rita Hayworth, or Jayne Mansfield in any number of films they never got to make. (Capitalism's endless prurience will most likely provide a variety of posthumous violations in our coming digital dystopia.) Hollywood will design completely unreal actresses and actors, made to computer specification. Because they will be chimeras, sprites, ghosts, they will be beings of complete and total spirit, but they will be devoid of soul, since one must first have a body to house such a thing. Because they are not human, they will leave no relics.

5 MEMORY

"*Handled already, Lord,*
clawed and clawing as though
the body of each of us were
your body, Lord."

— PAUL CELAN, "TENEBRAE"

Threaded underneath the cobble-stoned streets of Montparnasse is the empire of the dead. A necropolis where femurs and ribs, spines and skulls are all arrayed into patterns—crosses, arches, circles, spirals—across the walls of former quarries where limestone had been mined since the Romans. When fetid, overcrowded graveyards began to explode out from their retaining walls in the eighteenth-century, reposeful domains like the Saints-Innocent Cemetery and Saint-Etienne-des-Greces, the reigning Bourbons needed to find a new place to reinter the corpses. Fortuitously, the pliable Lutetian limestone mines from which the raw materials of the Louvre and

Notre Dame had been quarried were collapsing as of late, and so King Louis XVI in 1774 decided to use the bones of Parisians to fortify the bedrock of the city as it passed from the Medieval to the Modern and into the illuminations of Enlightenment. For two years starting in 1786, horse-drawn carriages berobed in black transported the exhumed bodies of the incalculable anonymous into the labyrinthine caves, anchoring contemporary Paris upon the fortifications of their ancestors.

This cadaverous construction, a purgatorial mine of around six million bodies (an ominous number for contemporary readers), meanders like veins beneath the flesh of the Left Bank, around sixty feet beneath Le Dome Café and Café de la Rotonde, the Dingo Bar and the Gallery of Montparnasse; there are the ossuaries of centuries of Parisian saints and sinners alike, all strangers to each other now. Affixed to the cave wall is some verse by the eighteenth-century dramatist Antoine-Marin Lemierre—"So many dead piled and pressed under the Earth! / Numbers here mean nothing; the crowd is lonely." On the surface, Montparnasse was where Amedeo Modigliani and Joan Miro composed their work, where F. Scott Fitzgerald and Ernest Hemingway wrote and drank, where exiled Leon Trotsky and Lenin conspired. But beneath are only the silent sepulchers of those forever quiet, their entrance and cenotaph reading "Stop! This is the Empire of Death!" To the living are given the streets, but everybody else must be content (though they are of course now nothing) with the caves below.

The pilgrim to Paris's macabre basement will perambulate on uneven, gravely ground, examining this gothic memento mori alongside the tinkle of freshwater draining through the natural limestone aquifers. Along the curved walls are the scaffolding of skull and bone. With a bit of bored whimsy, the eighteenth-century workers responsible for this cathedral of bones would organize the skulls of women and men into an undulating wave, or they would organize them into a cross. Marble memorial slabs from the demolished graveyards are inserted throughout this mass sculpture of human remains, and markers are left in granite informing the visitor of what cemetery these bodies were exhumed from, though all of the skeletons are now without name or identity. That is, in many ways, the most honest of explanations which the dead impart on us, for to see any skull is to see all skulls. "Paris has another Paris under herself," wrote Victor Hugo of the catacombs in *Les Misérables,* but the same is true of each of our masked faces, beneath which is the same skull.

While in matters of value and belief, ideology and meaning, we differ from these people who once dwelled for a bit in Paris—who loved, and worked, and prayed, and fucked, and created, and lived, through the reign of the Normans, the Valois, the Bourbons, the Jacobins—we at least share the most important thing. Beneath every face, beautiful or ugly, young or old, is the same smiling skull, and the innumerable forgotten of the Paris Catacombs attest to that inviolate axiom. "Wherever you go, death follows, a body's shadow" reads one marker nestled into the bones, the unnerving truth that we carry a skeleton with us always. Easy to mistake acknowledging the reality of death as rank nihilism, but it's the opposite. The catacombs don't entomb meaning, they feature an overabundance of it. Here, surrounded by the millions of the dead, their anonymity isn't the erasure of that which made them unique, rather it's a variety of deathly hallowed solidarity.

Despite all of the prurient interest which a visit to these caves might afford, it is a profoundly moving experience, a chorus not of the dead, but of the formerly living. "Fragile as men," reads a poem carved into a catacomb marker, "feeble as the void." Their remains are the bodily testament to the crucial fact that they were once here, that they once lived, that they were people. A demonstration of what it means to have a body, to share in their corporeality. Of my own visit to the catacombs, the most enduring memory isn't the skulls per se, but the thick, dusty, chalky coating of calcium carbonate stuck to the brown leather of my shoe, the mingled quintessence of a million dead, the atoms of Rabelais and Pascal, Racine and Lavoisier, their souls on my sole. Christine Quigley writes, in *Skulls and Skeletons: Human Bone Collections and Accumulations*, that "Unlike the Christian saints … the individual identities of the catacomb populace of Paris have remained anonymous." There are, to be sure, a multitude of the nameless saints beneath the streets of Paris; of women and men who treated the sick, tended the poor, and consoled the bereaved, regardless of whether or not they were canonized, but who are now part of the scaffolding of this underworld. There are also, to be sure, many sinners entombed beneath as well (for there are far more wicked than good people), noting that depending on one's political allegiance, the remains of Robespierre and Danton along with hundreds of their victims from the Reign of Terror are also beneath the sewers of the French capital, rather far from the mausoleum of the Pantheon. In a more elemental sense, the catacombs are a relic of humanity, of the *idea of humanity,* for mingled together, jumbled amidst each other's remains are the potent relics of the universal predicament.

If cemeteries exist to help us remember, the catacombs are a strange sort of cemetery, for nobody here has a name (save for one skull with the word "Fernando" carved into the bone). The sheer overwhelming numbers of these grounds are part of the reason; to be surrounded by the bones of six million, perhaps the largest assemblage of human remains on earth, is to be in the presence of the material divine. Awesome, sublime, transcendent. Also, obviously, horrifying. Many of those buried in the catacombs must have perished in the violent ways that people have always perished; there are victims of the Black Death, the Hundred Years War, the Wars of Religion, and the Reign of Terror all mixed together in the sterile earth. Many more perhaps lived relatively uneventful lives, happy ones even. This is not a memorial for the Black Death, the Hundred Years War, the Wars of Religion, or the Reign of Terror—this is an urban planning and civic improvement project. Memory isn't just obscured in the catacombs, it's not even the point. Despite that, the gathering of millions of the dead calls to mind less benign collections. To walk through the catacombs is to recall the pyre of charred skulls and femurs at Security Prison 21 in Phnom Penh, Cambodia; it's to see the bones of Nyamata Church some thirty miles south of Kigali, Rwanda, to look upon the white bleached fragments and shards dug from the fecund soil of Srebrenica, Bosnia. To walk among the six million dead of the catacombs is, rather obviously, to think of the six million murdered in the Holocaust. From Paris then there is the psychic resonance to the immolated of Dachau, Buchenwald, Auschwitz, transported from Berlin, Warsaw, Prague, and yes, also Paris. In reflecting upon the catacombs, there is the knowledge that everybody dies; in understanding the Holocaust, there is the wisdom which knows that not everybody dies the same death. Because of the sheer numbers of these places—the assembled bones in Cambodia, Rwanda, Bosnia, the exhaust of the ovens above Auschwitz—the mind is confronted with the enormity of memorialization. To make relics out of millions seems to be an impossibility, and yet in the bloodiest of centuries it paradoxically becomes even more morally imperative. When the organizers of the Tuol Sleng Genocide Museum preserve pyramids of skulls left by the Khmer Rouge, it's an acknowledgement of the failures of memory; when the curators of Kigali exhume mass graves and display those remains as clinically as a mortuary, it's to defer before the enormity of all which we can never know—personalities, identities, names. To acknowledge these remainders of a life not just as an artifact—or evidence—but also as a *relic* is to endow them with a sense of the divine, which is merely another way of saying the human.

Ours is the epoch of Holocaust and Hiroshima, concentration camp and gulag, where the nuclear sword of Damocles stands as coiled potential defining the most savage of human ages. As an ethical imperative there developed a very specific commandment—to bear witness. To remember. If memorials serve memory, then a heroic age demanded statues of heroes and sepulchers to founders, but such grandiosity rightly seems obscene in the age of the atom bomb and Auschwitz. Now, for those whose task it is to remember—not just historians, journalists, and educators, but architects, artists, city planners–they are also tasked with deciding how to memorialize events in which there are too many artifacts, when the horror of the century has seemingly rendered everybody and *every body* into a potential relic. In that staid, uniform, and drab neoclassical monument to pomposity that is Washington DC, there is a glaring exception in the form of the United States Holocaust Memorial Museum. Located on land not far from the obelisk of the Washington Memorial along the Potomac's reflecting pool, the museum's exterior as designed by architect James Ingo Freed appears like any number of other bureaucratic behemoths on the Mall. But the inside evokes the ghetto and extermination factories of the Nazis, all stark iron and shattered glass—depressing, disorienting, disturbing. Within there are liturgical objects and yellow stars, stripped camp uniforms and train boxcars; yet the most impacting exhibit is a massive pile of four thousand shoes. On permanent loan from the State Museum of Majdanek in Lublin, Poland, these are but a small portion of the staggering *three hundred thousand* shoes which belonged to women, children, and men gassed to death at Treblinka, Chelmno, and Auschwitz. There are cracked brown leather bluchers and black satin pumps, broken penny loafers and stained slippers. A pair of red, patent leather baby shoes. All that remains of these people, of their lives, are these material remnants, these relics, in a room permeated by the odor of rubber and the familiar smell of a person having just left the room.

If the gas chamber is the null point of modern history, those concrete rooms a moral void and singularity of meaninglessness into which millions of humans were sacrificed, then the crematorium is the belly of Moloch which took even the remains from us, the living, leaving behind only a pile of shoes. The raw materials themselves bear witness to what happened, and the elevation to such prosaic objects as a pair of wingtips or high heels to the level of relic is to try and remember those whose names we can never know as much as we are able to. The Nazis endeavored to reduce humans to things, in the most literal of senses. All of those horrific photographs of emaciated bodies dumped into deep trenches throughout the yards of the death camps; the images of storerooms full of shorn hair to be distributed as insulation in pillows for German soldiers on the eastern front. "They all died together," wrote Hannah Arendt in *Essays in Understanding, 1930-1954: Formation, Exile, and Totalitarianism,* "the young and old, the weak and the strong, the sick and the healthy; not as people, not as men and women, children and adults, boys and girls, not as good and bad, beautiful and ugly—but brought down to the lowest common denominator of organic life itself … like matter, like things that had neither body nor soul." Six million women, children, and men were immolated in Hitler's ovens, and along with them was incinerated any traditional image of God. When God is subtracted from faith, what remains? The relic. Because all of us share in the indignity of having a body, the basic atom of any true ethic must be based in materiality. To view portions of the body as a relic is to elevate it from mere thing, it is to try and undo what Arendt has diagnosed.

Our age is defined by those twin voids of the Holocaust and Hiroshima, both inculcated out of the same apocalyptic war. If God was incinerated in the crematoriums of the death camps, he was also immolated by the blast of the atomic bomb. Such murder on a grand, industrial, technological, scientific scale was literally unthinkable before the twentieth century; it is that barbarity and that barbarity alone which defines the conditions of modernity. Naturally, as its own variety of horrific theophany, Hiroshima has also produced remnants of people and their lives left after the blast, the role of the living now being to impart meaning out of this nothingness. Separated by multiple rivers and hills, Hiroshima Peace Memorial Park is situated on the island that was the hypocenter for the nuclear ground zero in 1945. Where once the survivors of the blast drowned in the flaming Motoyasu

River in an attempt to quench an unimaginable thirst, today the pilgrim walks past those embankments through the pastoral reverence of the park where the nuclear age began. The Hiroshima Peace Memorial Museum, an imposing steel and glass brutalist structure which dominates the park along with the shattered, twisted iron dome of the Prefectural Industrial Promotion Hall—one of the few structures to survive the explosion—is not just a place of education, but of reverence as well. Material artifacts of those who perished in the attack are appropriately afforded the status of relic; where objects were once made sacred by their proximity to divinity, now the dead Lord is rather expressed through the distance to something as horrible and sublime as the nuclear god.

Underneath plexiglass there is a charred wristwatch with a squarish face, the wrist on which it once sat burnt away in the blast, the arms of its face forever frozen at 8:15, the time in the morning when the bomb detonated. The tattered uniform of a junior high school student, the buttoned jacket stripped into long ribbons, the blue of the fabric singed brown at the edges. From the front of the Zen-oji Temple, only a bit more than a thousand feet from the hypocenter, there is an iron statue of the Buddha, melted from its face down to the base, hallowed out entirely, only the rough shape indicating what it may have once been. And then, as a relic of the true nihilism of modernity marked by industrialized war, there is the infamous "Human Shadow Etched in Stone." A quarter after 8 in the morning of August 6th, 1945 and somebody—some archivists believe it was a 43-year-old woman named Mitsuno Ochi—was sitting on the stone steps of the Sumitomo Bank, waiting for it to open, when the Americans dropped the bomb. With temperatures rising to over 4,000 degrees, she was vaporized, leaving behind a human shaped stain on the steps of the bank. A 1971 report published by the Hiroshima city government recorded that "people were killed almost immediately as if they had been vaporized … bodies and bones were burned throughout almost not to be found, and everything was destroyed, which was buried in white ash." How are we to be remembered if our bones don't even remain, if we're to be charred onto the concrete of the city, or expelled in the ash of a factory? If Hiroshima and the Holocaust killed God, they didn't kill the relic, for even if bones are reduced to dust and flesh is transformed into ash, human beings aren't just capable, but in fact required to preserve the idea of the relic. If there are no teeth or tongues, hair or bones to remember those who've been taken, then we will preserve shoes, we will preserve the steps on which they sat, and we will remember nonetheless.

A similar aura pervades the National Memorial for Peace and Justice in Montgomery, Alabama. Dedicated to the over four thousand mostly Black men lynched between the years 1877 (when Reconstruction ended) and 1950, and the memorial is an attempt to endow dignity and solemnity to those who were murdered by those who wished to uphold institutional white supremacy. At the museum, 805 steel rectangles representing each US county in which it's known that a lynching was committed hang above the visitor as if bodies from a poplar tree. For those whose names we know, they are recorded on the sides of each rectangle; for those whose names we don't know, allowances are made for the forgotten. Walking amongst these cenotaphs, the shape and size of hanging coffins, the exploitative gruesomeness of the act is replaced with quiet, mournful dignity—the impartation of a memorial service which the murdered were of course denied. Lynching is a particularly grotesque reduction of humanity, as a person is hanged, burnt, and often mutilated. An obscene sense of the carnivalesque often accompanied these hideous extrajudicial executions; dozens, hundreds, and sometimes even thousands of white citizens in mostly Southern towns would come to watch men (and sometimes women) be tortured, hanged, or burned alive. A photograph of Will Stanley's corpse, lynched in Temple, Texas in 1915, shows a burnt body scarcely recognizable as human anymore. On the back of a postcard commemorating this horror—a postcard—one of the murderers, named Joe Meyers, wrote to his parents—his parents—that "This is the Barbecue we had last night ... my picture is to the left." This killer, along with a dozen other men standing behind the charred remains of what had once been somebody's child.

The existence of lynching postcards, a particularly disturbing American invention, speaks to the way in which such murder reduced the body not just to artifact, but cruel entertainment. "During the slave regime, the Southern white man owned the Negro body and soul," wrote the journalist Ida B. Wells in her 1895 *Red Record.* "It was to his interest to dwarf the soul and preserve the body," the precise point of lynching as well, especially in what was ostensibly the post-slavery South. To hang a body, to mutilate a body, to burn a body, is to declare your inviolate ownership over that body, even beyond the dictates of economic instrumentalism which defined slavery itself. Yet the National Memorial for Peace and Justice attempts an act of sacred restoration on these bodies defiled, for even though there may be no remnants of the tortured left, the traces of their existence— as molecular as they may be—can still be preserved. Within the Legacy Museum, also in Montgomery and similarly dedicated to commemorating the victims of racial violence, there is an exhibit which features a multitude of jars filled with soil gathered at the sites of hundreds of lynchings. Lined up on a shelf as if they were spices or tea leaves, there is the rich, black soil of Phenix City, Alabama where Charles Humphries was killed in 1900, and brown pumice from Tampa, Florida where Robert Johnson was lynched in 1934, the red clay of Georgia and the Cecil soil of North Carolina. Bryan Stevenson, director of the Equal Justice Initiative which maintains the museums and memorial, explains that "In the soil there is the blood of victims of racial violence and lynching. There are tears in the soil from all those who labored under … indignation and humiliation." Slavery may have reduced the body to commodity and lynching to cruel spectacle, but the act of memory restores it to the status of a relic. By displaying a simple jar of dirt there is an act of audacious resistance. There may no longer be full bodies left to bury, but in the soil with its intermingled atoms of blood and tears, there is a sense that despite it all, the *human* still remains.

In my own city of Pittsburgh, four blocks from where I now write, there is the site of martyrdom where eleven Jews were murdered, the largest pogrom in American history. Tree of Life Synagogue, a lodestar of Pittsburgh's large Jewish population, was clothed in granite, with massive, modernist stained-glass windows that faced Shady Avenue. When a white supremacist entered that sanctuary with a Colt AR-15 on October 27th, 2018, it was not just an evil, but a violation of sacred ground. The intent of such evil—and let us not pretend that such things can be reduced to mere sociology or biochemistry—is to undo the world, to erase the human. To murder somebody is to assault the body, but it's also to attempt to destroy the soul, for those two are inextricably connected. From the horror of the Tree of Life massacre, those who are living did what is always to be done—to preserve what can be preserved and to ensure that the memory of those taken should endure as a blessing.

Writing for *Tablet Magazine,* Shira Telushkin explains how as concerns the victims, "their blood cannot be forgotten, simply scrubbed away and disposed of. It must be honored, collected, and buried." Telushkin describes the role of chevra kadisha, a Jewish burial society that makes sure that all of the remains are accounted for, a group which included "three rabbis, two medics, a painter, and a doctor." Though members of the Jewish community, they weren't necessarily members of the congregation, and they didn't necessarily know those who were killed. The work is strenuous. The work is horrifying. And yet chevra kadisha continued, for it is what is owed to humans. My neighbors who were murdered in Tree of Life were not evidence and they were not simply matter, they were people. By treating the body with reverence, by showing remains such respect, it is a consummate enactment of relic logic, a demonstration of how honoring what is holy of the body is to honor what is good in the soul. As concerns God and the prophets, heaven and the saints, I am often studiously agnostic; but that we all share in this corporeal life, that we all have bodies which often are in pain but that can also feel pleasure, that ache, twinge, throb, and hurt, but which also know the contentment of a nap, the comforts of a meal, the consolations of an embrace, the love of holding our children, is an irrefutable reality. If our embodiment is the source of our ethics, it must be born from an awareness that human hands can kill, but that they can also gather the remains of strangers as an act of love. Whether or not there is a God has no relationship to if we are to be good, for that we have our sisters and brothers is justification enough. If you fear that there is a hell, it is in the space where man has enacted such violence on his fellow suffering humans. If you pray that there is a heaven, it is in the place where suffering humans work, hand in hand, to rebuild that world again.

INDEX

The Object Lessons series achieves something very close to magic: the books take ordinary—even banal—objects and animate them with a rich history of invention, political struggle, science, and popular mythology. Filled with fascinating details and conveyed in sharp, accessible prose, the books make the everyday world come to life. Be warned: once you've read a few of these, you'll start walking around your house, picking up random objects, and musing aloud: 'I wonder what the story is behind this thing?'"

Steven Johnson, author of *Where Good Ideas Come From* and *How We Got to Now*

Object Lessons describes themselves as 'short, beautiful books,' and to that, I'll say, amen. ... If you read enough Object Lessons books, you'll fill your head with plenty of trivia to amaze and annoy your friends and loved ones—caution recommended on pontificating on the objects surrounding you. More importantly, though... they inspire us to take a second look at parts of the everyday that we've taken for granted. These are not so much lessons about the objects themselves, but opportunities for self-reflection and storytelling. They remind us that we are surrounded by a wondrous world, as long as we care to look."

John Warner, *The Chicago Tribune*

The joy of the series, of reading *Remote Control*, *Golf Ball*, *Driver's License*, *Drone*, *Silence*, *Glass*, *Refrigerator*, *Hotel*, and *Waste* (more titles are listed as forthcoming) in quick succession, lies in encountering the various turns through which each of their authors has been put by his or her object. As for Benjamin, so for the authors of the series, the object predominates, sits squarely center stage, directs the action. The object decides the genre, the chronology, and the limits of the study. Accordingly, the author has to take her cue from the *thing* she chose or that chose her. The result is a wonderfully uneven series of books, each one a *thing* unto itself."

Julian Yates, *Los Angeles Review of Books*

The Object Lessons series has a beautifully simple premise. Each book or essay centers on a specific object. This can be mundane or unexpected, humorous or politically timely. Whatever the subject, these descriptions reveal the rich worlds hidden under the surface of things."

Christine Ro, *Book Riot*

... a sensibility somewhere between Roland Barthes and Wes Anderson."

Simon Reynolds, author of *Retromania: Pop Culture's Addiction to Its Own Past*

My favourite series of short pop culture books"

Zoomer magazine